No Need to Kill Fleas with a Gun

Tales of a drug mule girl in Ciudad Juárez

DESARTICULACIONES
Colección
Homenaje a Silvia Molloy

Homage to Silvia Molloy
Collection
BREAK UP

Jacqueline Loweree

No Need to Kill Fleas with a Gun

Tales of a drug mule girl in Ciudad Juárez

Nueva York Poetry Press

Nueva York Poetry Press LLC
128 Madison Avenue, Oficina 2NR
New York, NY 10016, USA
Teléfono: +1(929)354-7778
nuevayork.poetrypress@gmail.com
www.nuevayorkpoetrypress.com

No Need to Kill Fleas with a Gun
Tales of a drug mule girl in Ciudad Juárez

© 2025, Jacqueline Loweree

ISBN-13: 978-1-966772-70-5

© Break up Collection
Colección Desarticulaciones vol. 2
Non Fiction- Otros discursos
(Homenaje a Sylvia Molloy)

© Publisher:
Marisa Russo

© Editor:
Francisco Trejo

© Layout Designer:
Moctezuma Rodríguez

© Cover Designer:
William Velásquez Vásquez

© Translation:
Jacqueline Loweree

© Cover Image and Illustrations:
Miguel Asa

Loweree, Jacqueline
No Need to Kill Fleas with a Gun. Tales of a drug mule girl in Ciudad Juárez / Jacqueline Loweree; 1ª ed. New York: Nueva York Poetry Press, 2025. 158 pp. 13.97 X 21.59.

1. Mexican Literature   2. Latin American Literature

All rights reserved. No part of this publication may be reproduced, distributed, or transmitted in any form or by any means, including photocopying, recording, or other electronic or mechanical methods, without the prior written permission of the publisher, except in the case of brief quotations emboied in critical reviews and certain other non-commercial uses permitted by copyright law. For permissions contact the publisher at: nuevayork.poetrypress@gmail.com.

To my mom.

Author's Note

Not long ago, a friend of mine wrote to ask me for a poem. He intended to publish it in the second issue of a literary magazine that had just debuted in Madrid. I tend to be fairly committed when it comes to poetic requests from friends, so I acquiesced and asked if the magazine had a theme.

"The topic is open, but I'd love it if you could send me something about Juárez, about your life there," he replied by email.

His proposal, somewhat unexpected, weighed on me for days. It is true that I responded right away with a resounding "of course". It is true that the idea of sending him a piece about my city for a mostly Spanish audience was exciting. Little is known about Juárez internationally beyond the usual: drug trafficking, violence, femicides, and migration. But it is also true that I felt a knot in my stomach as I read those words on my phone screen. I had absolutely no idea what poem I could send him, already written, about my city.

I am a writer, or rather, a poet, which is the same in the end, but not professionally, let us say recreationally. I have the unfortunate habit of writing honestly through verse, and far from becoming a "little goddess"[1], I make myself mortal before the reader's (or the listener's in the case of poetry) insatiable critique. I write about living with bipolar disorder, sometimes explicitly, sometimes

---

[1] Little god[des] refers to a verse from a poem by Vicente Huidobro

implicitly, and I advocate for restraints on judgment and greater understanding through my writing.

So, the idea of sending a poem about a place I had not visited in years, one that did not quite fit into my usual leitmotif, made me nauseous. I started combing through my books frantically, seeking any mention of Juárez in my work. But the more I flipped through dozens of pages, the more I realized that this part of my life, at least in my writing, was noticeably undernourished.

I am an immigrant, though perhaps due to generalizations about the population, I am an atypical one. I was born in the United States, but as soon as my mom was discharged from the hospital, we crossed the border heading south. I was raised sucking on Vero-brand watermelon lollipops with Tajín, not Dum Dums from the U.S., and eating *chile relleno* burritos and tortas de *colita de pavo* slathered in spicy salsa, not McDonald's or ham-and-Kraft-cheese sandwiches. I grew up being an American citizen in Mexico without speaking a single word of English, or, as I describe in one of my stories, I am a *juareñita americanser*.

It is worth noting that there has been, and still is, an identity complex throughout my life. To be clear, the complex is not mine. I know perfectly well who I am, where I come from, and the cultural values I was raised with. The complex belongs to others, those who cannot fit me into their established paradigms, simply because they cannot visualize a culture that is not monolithic. To some, I have been, am, and will always be a bewildering contrast.

When I was in university, I had a professor who later became the chair of my thesis committee, Dr. Campbell, a devilish anthropologist with an air of Anthony Bourdain. He became one of the most well-known American academics for his social studies on Mexican drug trafficking. Without a doubt, the professor had thoroughly studied me.

I remember once making my way to his office and running into a tough-looking guy at his door with a "don't look at me, don't touch me" kind of face. They asked me to wait a few minutes, closed the door, and I sat on the hallway stairs awaiting my turn. Finally, when the professor was free, he welcomed me with a laugh.

"I crack up when I think that this guy with his gangster face, but from a 'good' family, wants to study drug trafficking in Mexico. And you, with your sweet face but that life of yours, have no intention of engaging in the reality you lived," he said.

And here is my confession, and the connection to my friend's literary request: I cannot write about Ciudad Juárez, not with my sincere habit, without speaking of drug trafficking, of grinding poverty, and of violence against women. Unfortunately, and truthfully, these topics are intertwined, at least for me and for many other *juarenses*. In the nineties, we experienced the economic boom of the *maquiladoras*[2], waves of migration from the south, the unstoppable rise in femicides, the consolidation of the Juárez Cartel's power over the region as a strategic gateway abroad, and poverty embodied in the growing informal settlements on the city's outskirts. Our beloved border transformed during that decade, eventually becoming the most dangerous city in the world.

I subtitled the book *Tales of a drug mule girl in Ciudad Juárez*, not metaphorically, but because that is precisely what they are. I was a child entangled in the entrails of an underworld that, for many, became its daily bread, or tortilla, in our case, and for others, its violent and most despicable ruin. For us, that life was a necessity, a survival mechanism, call it what you will, labels be damned. Later, due to other, but also survival-related, circumstances, we fled and left that world behind entirely. I longed to forget it. I tried to rebuild my life and move forward. And I did. I studied, and through my own efforts, climbed out of that crushing poverty. I moved far away to become a person, at least a "normal" one, whatever that means. But childhood always leaves behind a thorn, and the more you try to reject it, the deeper it buries itself.

Then someone asks you to write about that life you tried to drown, you, the honest one, and the thorn mutates into a blade you can no longer ignore.

---

[2] Factories located in Mexico, owned by foreign parties

That is how *No Need to Kill Fleas with a Gun* was born, a book written from the perspective of a quiet, brave, soft-hearted girl where the border, "the most beautiful and lovely city in the world", becomes a recurring character symbolizing struggle, described across ten true stories. The book is an act of rescued memory, a kind of retrospective reconciliation, narrated almost anthropologically, with events and characters based on real life, except for the occasional fictional name.

It is worth clarifying that drug trafficking and structural violence are not the protagonists here, but rather the unnecessary conditions and lack of options that lead thousands of families into difficult situations, turning them into lives filled with anecdotes, sayings, food, laughter, and yes, in many cases, relentless tears. This reality is absurd, simply because no one in Mexico, a country of abundance, should be cornered into choosing between the sharpness of a sword and the precipice of a cliff just to survive. But when all you have is a pistol and a flea-sized problem, shooting fleas to kill them starts to make sense.

*Knife city.
Infamy on every map,
its cut clean.*

*Ciudad cuchillo.
En los mapas la infamia,
su corte limpio.*

Haikus of Ciudad Juárez
María Ángeles Pérez López

Pakas de a kilo en el gabacho

BUNDLES OF CONTRABAND IN THE 'GABACHO'[3]

Goodbye, sierras of Coahuila,
Of Sinaloa and Durango,
Of Sonora and Tamaulipas,
Chihuahua, you're here to stay,
If you want to find me now,
In Juárez I'm out and about.

Pacas de a kilo by LOS TIGRES DEL NORTE

Three bloodied and muddied fingers smeared on the windowpane were the last trace of my stepfather before he fled the house. At last, the wail of ambulances and the racket of nosy neighbors had settled. Everything was quiet now, but in disarray. The house looked as if a category six hurricane had torn through it. Broken furniture, an emptied pantry, filthy and clean clothes flung like confetti everywhere, shattered glass, blood, in puddles and streaked across the walls. It looked like a crime scene straight out of an episode of *Law & Order*. In a way, it was.

My mom had tried to calm him down. First, by speaking to him gently, then by being direct, until finally by breaking into tears and begging him, followed by hitting him, and ending with the most desperate act of all: stabbing her own leg with a

---

[3] Term used in Mexico to describe foreigners (or a foreign place), particularly those from the United States, usually in a derogatory way

knife. All in the hopeless attempt to snap him out of his trance. But he was already too far gone.

Feeling cornered by my mother like a sheep about to be torn into shreds by a wolf, he grabbed a bat and started smashing everything in his path. Cabinets, chairs, picture frames, the television, and finally the glass doors leading to the patio. Like a wild animal, he picked up a shard of glass with his cinnamon-colored hand.

"Get the fuck out of my way or I'll mess you up!" he threatened.

Blood from his right hand slid down his wrist, dripping in steady streams that pooled in stark contrast against the gleaming white ceramic floor. I did not know what to do. I looked at him, then at my mother. Both were in a state of frenzy, in a sort of duel; she, desperate to stabilize him; he, frantic to escape. Both were bleeding.

Just then, the wail of ambulance and police sirens interrupted the Mexican standoff between my parents. The neighbors, who were used to living in a quiet and seemingly boring neighborhood, had taken the liberty of calling 911, maybe for the first time in their miserable lives.

Without missing a beat, my stepfather bolted down the hallway toward the back room and jumped out the window, flinging himself into the frigidity of December completely naked.

What happened next feels hazy. I remember hearing my mother's scream and watching her hurriedly get dressed, while limping on her left leg. I remember stepping barefoot onto the sidewalk, blinded by the dazzling lights of the police car. I remember seeing my stepfather restrained by two burly men in navy-blue uniforms, pistols hanging from their belts. I remember the back door of the ambulance swung open and watching as my stepfather was strapped onto a stretcher, wounded, but already sedated. I remember the neighbors, my friends whom I used to play baseball with, shocked and wide-eyed. Nothing would ever be the same again. The illusion of being a normal family in the *Uniteds* had come crashing down.

Seeing me standing there, almost in a daze, Paula, my friend from across the street, walked over, extended her hand, and returned the Barbie I had left at her house just before all had unfolded.

"Hey, my mom says it's better if we don't play anymore... and that you shouldn't come over," she said.

With that blunt declaration, I felt like the black sheep of the block, humiliated, exposed to the judgment of the saints who pelted me with stones through their prying and righteous stares.

I did not even have time to cry, because in the blink of an eye, the ambulance and patrol cars had dissipated. My mother, still limping but resolute, smiled at the onlookers as if she were onstage in a play with a tragic ending, covering the gap where her lateral incisor used to be with her tongue, as she generally did. I had always thought my mother to be a shy woman, but later I realized it was not shyness, rather caution, her mechanism to avoid making a scene and drawing attention. I imagine her performance of normalcy was also a way to salvage what little was left of her dignity.

When we walked back into the house and were struck by the crime scene, we found my younger siblings hiding in the hallway bathroom. Swallowing her tears, my mom sat us down on the floor since most of the chairs had been smashed to protruding pieces. She proceeded to explain what was about to take place.

First, we were going to scrub the entire house with bleach, especially the bathroom sinks. We could not leave a single trace. Then my mom and I would haul down the hundred kilos of contraband we kept hidden in a hole in the master-bedroom closet wall. My siblings, meanwhile, would gather every bit of dirty laundry and carry it to the garage. We would load the bundles one by one into the trunk of the station wagon, one of those ancient, wood-paneled models, and cover them with the piles of clothes my siblings had stacked up.

At last, when I had mopped the final crusted streak of blood clinging stubbornly to the pale ceramic floor, the clock struck midnight. Running on pure adrenaline and the fear that the police might return "to ask questions", our mom fixed us dinner. She warmed some beans she had stored in the fridge inside a tan Country Crock margarine tub. With the practiced ease of years in the kitchen, she spread the beans over three flour tortillas, rolled them up, and handed each of us a bean burrito. She did not eat. Five minutes later she grabbed me by the arm and told me to ride shotgun in the wagon while she put my siblings to bed.

We slipped out of the garage around 12:25. The streets of El Paso at that hour were mostly empty, except for the occasional partygoer acting like a *vergas*[4] behind the wheel. It was precisely because of the drunk drivers that we had to be extra careful. Trying to meet their quotas, the cops were out on the prowl, hunting for any sinner rolling on motorized rubber.

Without traffic and with a steady gauge on the speed limit, our destination was about twenty-five minutes away. We did not murmur a single word the entire ride. But every so often, I could hear my mother blow her nose while she wiped away tears with the sleeve of her jacket so she could keep clear sight of the road.

The hundred kilo bundles, hidden beneath t-shirts and filth-crusted socks, seemed to double in weight as we merged onto I-10, the city's main highway. After about seven agonizing minutes, we eased into the right lane and took the Lee Trevino exit, heading toward the Lower Valley.

The Lower Valley was considered the city's countryside, where urban growth still bowed to farmland

---

[4] Mexican slang for saying "badass"

rather than strip malls. Most houses, varied in size and color, camouflaged behind rusty iron fencing and stone and concrete walls. In this rural patch on the south-central edge of town, it was routine to run into livestock ambling down the streets.

As my mom swung into the last alley, she slammed on the brakes, and, with no seat belt, I smacked face-first into the station-wagon's dashboard. At that hour of the pre-dawn, a duck and her ducklings decided to waddle across the road in a single file, in no evident rush. We cut the engine and waited. The only sounds in that low valley were those of the crickets and the soft *quack-quack* of the familial promenade.

For the first time all day, I heard my mom burst into laughter at the sheer absurdity of it all. In my head I pictured a news headline: "Woman with knife wound and her nine-year-old daughter stopped by a family of ducks while smuggling one hundred kilos of cocaine wrapped in dirty laundry".

"We're nearly there, it's all the way at the end," my mother said, as the line of ducklings faded into the bushes.

The house sat at the end of the driveway, tucked behind a tall gate in the front yard. We slipped in without trouble with my mom's key. In the dim moonlight, the house revealed its soft yellow glow, giving the impression of a mansion. Not a single light could be perceived through the windows.

"I'm getting out and it may take a while," she warned. "Keep an eye on the clock, and if more than twenty minutes go by, sneak out, run, and find a cop."

There was no time for me to assimilate her instructions. In a flash, she vanished into the shadows cast by the pecan trees, leaving only the scent of confusion behind. Run and find the police, but why? Were we not running from them? And where was I supposed to get a phone at this time? Instinctively my body began to shake, not from the cold this time, but from panic about what might be happening to my mom in that house while the minutes blinked past on the dashboard clock.

Wiping away a bead of sweat that slid down my forehead and blurred my vision, I made out the silhouettes of three people, one of them limping. They moved in feline-like, my mother and two men in boots, loose-faded jeans, sporting thick mustaches. They clicked on two flashlights and began shining their beams across the back of the wagon, inspecting the bundles of clothes.

"It's all wrapped up in the clothes," my mother said, pointing with one hand. "But the hundred are all there."

They took longer to unwrap and count each kilo than we had taken to hide them. To me, they looked like two impatient kids vehemently tearing into their Christmas presents, only to wind up utterly disappointed. When they finally reached the last bundle, they gave my mother the signal that everything checked out and that we could go. We pulled away without saying goodbye, tempted to slam the gas pedal but heedful not to make a sound that might betray us in the thick silence. The car, like the tension in the air, felt noticeably lighter.

The clock read three in the morning when we opened the garage door. My mom climbed out of the wagon and, the moment her foot touched the concrete, she collapsed with a howl. The pain in her left leg, numbed for hours by adrenaline, returned with vengeance, and this time she could not ignore it. Desperate, watching her writhing on the ground, I had no idea what to do, so I fetched a wet rag to tie around the wound. I had zero clue what I was doing; I only remembered that in the movies they wrapped injuries with whatever scrap of cloth was at hand.

"What are you doing?!" she screamed as I tried to grab her leg. "No, move. Help me up. Get me in the car. You'll have to drive."

Her plan was that we would head to the hospital and that I, a nine-year-old who had never touched a steering wheel, would drive, because she was about to faint from the pain. The sweat returned, this time in torrents.

"Don't worry, I'll tell you what to do, just pay close attention."

I grabbed her by the waist and helped her up, nearly dragging her into the passenger seat. She was crying. Tears were falling from my eyes, too, but at that moment, I had to be strong, I could not afford the luxury of falling apart. I climbed into the driver's seat and followed, step by step, every instruction she gave me between sobs.

Insert the key. Turn it forward until it starts. Press the brake. Shift into reverse. Let go of the brake. Press the gas, slowly, not too slowly! You are doing fine, do not worry. Now, hit the brakes again. Shift into first. Go. A little faster now. Put on your blinker. You are going to turn here. Keep going until the stop sign, and brake, not so hard! Go again. We are almost there. You are doing great. Turn in here. Park over there.

We made it to the hospital without any notable issues, just a few sudden accelerations and jerky stops. Once in the parking lot, proud of my accomplishment as a first-time driver, I turned off the engine with a sly smile, pulled out the keys, got out, and opened the passenger door to help my mother out. She was unconscious.

What happened next is a blur. I know I ran to the hospital entrance. I know I saw my mother lying on a stretcher. I know the nurses offered me food while I waited in a brightly lit room full of curtains and beeping machines. I know I did not eat. I know I curled up across two chairs and laid there in a ball. That is the last thing I remember from that nightmare.

The length of my nap remains an unknown, but I do know that when I woke up, I saw my mother lying in front of me. Several intravenous lines were connected to her arm, and her leg hung bandaged and completely exposed. Still half-asleep and disoriented, I could not fully assimilate the entirety of the scene that unfolded around the bed.

A woman, older, with her hair neatly pulled back and dressed elegantly, was sitting beside my mother, the two of them were speaking softly. Like me, she was waiting at the hospital while her husband was in surgery. She had seen me asleep across the chairs and decided to sit with my mother so as not to disturb my nap.

When she noticed I had awakened, my mom smiled desolately and with just the lead of her gaze, she introduced me to the woman.

"Look, *mija*, this is Doña Emilia. Her husband got sick," she said. "I told her you were brave, that you brought me to the hospital."

In lieu of the expected pleasantries, I said nothing more than a quiet "hello" and quickly excused myself to go to the restroom. Doña Emilia took the opportunity to walk with me down the long hallway. "Take good care of her," she said as we reached the doors leading to the exit. She took my hand and slipped a rolled-up bill into it, "So you two can get something to eat."

When I finally exited the restroom and scanned the hallway looking for that generous woman, I realized she was gone. I never saw her again. The rolled-up bill burned in my pocket. I pulled it out, it was twenty whole dollars, probably the largest bill I had ever seen in person. With that, we could buy a whole week's worth of groceries.

A few hours later my mom was discharged. As we stepped into the parking lot, the morning sun blinded us. When we got home, Isela and Andrés were still tucked away dreaming. The house smelled distinctly of a mix of bleach and the lingering stench of old lard crusted into a skillet that was left on the stove.

Ignoring the whirlwind of the night before, I headed straight to the back room, the one that had been assigned to me. It had nothing but a twin mattress on the floor and a plastic bin pushed up against the wall to serve as a dresser, with a small makeshift mirror propped on top. I collapsed onto the mattress undisturbed until one p.m.

It was December twenty-fourth, and it was snowing, the first snowfall I had ever witnessed. In the desert, our winters could cut straight through to the bone, but snow had always been something from "somewhere else" something out of the movies. But that day, the white blanket of snowflakes piling up in the yard stood in a stark, and much-needed, contrast to the darkness inside the house.

My siblings were already outside, making the most of the extraordinary event, while my mom busied herself in the kitchen. We both knew that despite the unexpected meteorological gift, we had no tree, no *tamales* or *champurrado*, and no presents for the kids to celebrate Christmas eve.

"What if we go with *los chinos*?" I asked, suddenly remembering the twenty-dollar miracle from Doña Emilia.

"Los chinos" referred to the discount stores full of cheap, mostly disposable goods that were everywhere in downtown El Paso. I never knew if the nickname came from the merchandise being imported from China or because the owners themselves were Chinese. What was certain, however, was that twenty dollars at one of those stores could buy just enough to create the semblance of a decent Christmas, minus the *tamales* and *champurrado*.

Piled into the station wagon once again, the four of us headed downtown. I remember we stopped at the first dollar store we stumbled upon. My mom went in with the bill and soon came back out with a yellow plastic bag. Sitting in the driver's seat, she opened the bag and started pulling out tiny items, calling out each of our names like we were all gathered in one of my aunt's living rooms during a Christmas gift exchange celebration.

As I heard my name being called, I saw a tiny notebook-shaped keychain emerging from the plastic bag, complete with its own tiny pencil, "for you, Jacqueline, because you love to write". I held out my hand and took it, curious to inspect the small object.

Nine days later ICE deported my stepfather. So, we had to flee the house and return to Juárez. The *jefes de jefes*[5] blamed my mom for stealing a hundred kilos of cocaine. The two thick-mustached men never reported that pre-dawn delivery, turning

---

[5] The title of a song from Los Tigres del Norte translating to the "bosses' bosses"

the fate of those drugs into a stolen mystery. Therefore, staying in that El Paso house was no longer safe.

As far as I was concerned, we faced three threats. First, imminent eviction: no cocaine, no deal, and the deal covered the rent. Second, the police: after my stepfather was arrested and then deported, we knew they would be back to investigate. He had been detained because he had was under the severe effects of a drug overdose and deported because he had no papers. Third, and most frightening, the traffickers themselves, demanding their hundred kilos of contraband.

With little time to pack, we carried back just the essentials. Between my clothes and my schoolbooks, I made sure to tuck away my new keychain. I was ready to leave behind our first attempt at life in the *Uniteds* and return to Ciudad Juárez, with our tail between our legs.

> *Goodbye, [the desert] of [the Uniteds],*
> *Of [El Paso] and the [Lower Valley],*
> *Of [ICE] and the [white gabachos],*
> *Chihuahua, you're here to stay,*
> *If you want to find me now,*
> *In Juárez I'm out and about.*
>
> *Pacas de a kilo*
> of LOS TIGRES DEL NORTE and the AUTHOR

POR UNA MEADA, UN BURJERO

ALL 'CAUSE OF A PISS, A BURRERO

The *tortería*[6] sat at the intersection of two major avenues. A modest, unremarkable one-story building, its façade was adorned with freshly painted signs proclaiming the best tortas in Ciudad Juárez. What set the place apart, however, and gave it local renown, was its circular shape and green awning. Perhaps that is why the lunchtime crowds often spilled out into the sidewalk. One could say that the *tortería* enjoyed a certain popularity, though it was never entirely clear whether that stemmed from the tortas truly living up to their hype, from its strategic location, or simply from the novelty of its architecture. What was certain, however, was that its success owed nothing to the "charm" of its owner.

A robust and uninviting man, the owner was known simply as *Moy el Tortero*. In truth, no one really knew his actual name, nor whether he had a family, let alone children. He was the kind of person who inspired both fear and bewilderment. Fear, because his demeanor was anything but courteous, veering instead toward the openly hostile. He would erupt into sharp outbursts, barking orders whenever the ceiling fan began to wobble from overuse, or whenever Juan Gabriel played on the radio.

---

[6] Shop where Mexican style tortas, or sandwiches, are prepared

"Fucking *nacos lentejueleados*[7]!" he would shout, referring to the radio DJs.

I found it comical how his apron, thoroughly stained with grease, would soak through with sweat as he would dash over to the radio to violently wrench the dial to the left whenever the "bastards" at the station dared to play another Juan Gabriel tune. At the age of seven, I could not fathom why he harbored such contempt for the singer. In fact, to me, *El Divo de Juárez*, with his sequined suits, and *Moy el Tortero*, with his grimy aprons, shared a few physical traits and mannerisms, let us say, somewhat flamboyant. Though one was charming in demeanor, and the other one was a sweaty type of ogre.

And yet, and here is where the confusion is evidenced, Moy also harbored a kind of empathy, though it was meticulously concealed and rationed to very few. A natural-born skeptic, Moy preferred to work alone, but when he first launched his business, he had no choice but to hire help. He had known my parents for years and, though begrudgingly and driven more by necessity than goodwill, he offered them a weekend gig.

"I'll give you fifty pesos a day, and put the girl to work too, so she's not just loafing around!" Moy declared.

"Come on, *compadre*, fifty doesn't even cover bus fare, and there's three of us," my stepdad bargained.

---

[7] Refers to those who listen to Juan Gabriel, an iconic Mexican singer, renowned for his indirect representation of the LGTQIA+ community; a derogatory term translating loosely to "low lives in sequin"

"Well, it's fifty pesos a day or nothing, up to you," Moy replied.

Things were rough in our neck of our woodless desert, so we had no choice but to accept his third-world deal. A few months earlier, we had been evicted of the apartment we were renting over in La Satélite, and we had been living mostly out of our car ever since, a beat-up '80s Jeep Cherokee, a real Frankenstein of a ride that shed parts every time we turned it on. Sometimes the muffler would fall off, other times the front bumper. We could not even afford gas anymore. So, when Moy hurled that exploitation disguised in charity at us, we snatched it without complaints, nor questions, and got to work from sunup to sundown.

During those long summer days, lengthened in the cradle of the desert, when even the walls sweat, the three of us kept the *tortería* afloat, always under Moy's militaristic vigilance, who made damn sure none of us dared eat a torta without paying for it first. While my parents took orders, sliced bread, and packed rolls with *colitas de pavo*[8] and avocado, I became *La Tráeme*[9], "bring me a bucket", "bring me the sodas from the cooler", "bring me the salsa", "bring me the mop". Additionally, I played the role of *La Hazte*[10] "make yourself invisible", "make

---

[8] Typical dish, generally prepared in a torta, in Juárez translating to "turkey tails"
[9] The "bring me"
[10] The "make yourself"

yourself out of the way", "make yourself dumb", "make yourself like you didn't see a thing".

That last role, *La Hazte*, was especially important, because there were strange happenings that, at that age, I could not explain, let alone speak about out loud. Every now and then, men would show up at the *tortería*, hard-faced, suspicious-looking types, asking for the boss. Their eyes usually evaded mine, even though I was the one ringing them up. They seemed rushed, like they did not want to be there a second longer than necessary. Moy would then emerge, jittery, from his closet-sized office, completely brushing us off, and without a word would walk out with his visitor toward the parking lot down the corner. Several hours later he would return seemingly off and absent-minded. We used those absences to prepare ourselves some tortas, utterly ignoring the boss's mandate to open the register and deposit the required twenty pesos.

"Who are those men, and what does Moy do with them?" I once asked my mother.

"You do not judge what you can see, *mija*," she replied.

It is worth noting that Moy, because he was unpleasant or perhaps a bit effeminate, was an easy target in a dusty sea of macho and insecure Mexican men. There was a general sense of rivalry among the nearby vendors, but one feud stood out: the one with the *burrero*[11] from the shop in the back, a tall, broad,

---

[11] Person who sells burritos

dark-skinned man who sold burritos from a little three-meter stall. But business was not exactly booming for him. For every ten customers who showed up at the *tortería*, maybe one bought a burrito. He never made conversation nor smiled. Ever cautious, I would try to avoid crossing paths with the *burrero*, but every now and then I would catch sight of him hauling boxes to dump behind the *tortería*. Moy would fly into a rage when he saw his turf littered with greasy cardboard, tin cans, and empty Sabritas' wrappers. With fists clenched, he would storm over to the *burrero's* stall, cursing him out at the top of his lungs, furiously stabbing each step on the blistering asphalt. Then came the cacophony of two old street vendors locked in a shouting match fit for a street market battlefield.

One Friday, around eight in the morning, as we rushed off the *rutera*[12] across the avenue, we noticed a strange scene. The *tortería* was completely shut, and it looked unusually neglected, the sidewalks out front had not been swept in days. Even after knocking several times, we received nothing but silence emanating from within. We waited until lunchtime, each of us offering our own theory about Moy's odd disappearance. As much of an ogre as he was, the guy had never missed a day of work, and he was never late.

"What if he left with one of those men who used to come looking for him before we got here?" I asked.

---

[12] The public buses prevalent in Ciudad Juárez

"I doubt it. This is strange, but let's wait, we don't have a dime to get back with," my mom replied.

Growing restless, I had no idea how much longer we would have to stand guard. The heat kept climbing, and without that wobbly old fan, sweat began to melt down my forehead. By the time all three of us were in the "don't touch me, don't look at me" mood, we suddenly heard a distant shout coming from the parking attendant from the corner lot.

"*Q'ubole, carnal*[13], how's it going?" asked the parking guy.

"Well, we've been here waiting on Moy, seems like the bastard went on a bender," my stepdad said.

"Ah, *compadre*... you didn't hear? Word is, Moy kicked the bucket," said the attendant.

"What are you saying? What happened to him?" asked my stepdad in complete awe.

When invited to speak, the parking attendant straightened his back with a theatrical flair, as if gearing up for his afternoon performance, eyes gleaming with morbid curiosity. He began recounting the tragic fate of *Moy el Tortero*.

"Well look, Tuesday I was in a damn rush 'cause my old lady couldn't make it to work with me," he started. "It wasn't even eleven when we heard this wailing, like a dog or something, and I thought, 'Ah, hell, who's gettin' their ass kicked now?' Then suddenly,

---

[13] Slang translating to "what's up, man?"

all the guys around here started running, and, well, I went right along with 'em."

"Listen, *compadre*, when I got close, I saw Moy, laid out and covered in blood. I mean, already dead," he added, pausing for dramatic effect.

"But what happened?" my stepdad pressed.

"Well, turns out Moy had gone lookin' for trouble, and the bastard decided to take a piss right next to the burrito stand. That *pinche* caveman heard him and came out fuming. Gave him a beating. I don't know if it was 'cause he was a pain in the ass or just 'cause he was a *puto*[14], but that *burrero* took it out on him," he explained.

"You're telling me the *burrero* beat the guy to death over damn piss, *compadre*?" my stepdad asked.

"That's right, 'cause of a piss, *compadre*," the parking guy declared.

Moy was buried a week later. Turns out he did have family, a white-haired aunt and two devoutly Catholic sisters. We attended the wake, held in a small-stuffy house with closed windows and overcrowded with sacred objects. Moy was the first dead body I ever saw, at age seven. Every time I hear Juan Gabriel now, I think of Moy. I get a little sad. Now I understand.

---

[14] Derogatory way of calling a man gay

DE MULA EN LOS CERROS DE ALTAVISTA

A Mule in the Hills
of Altavista

The truck, or La Pandita, as we had nicknamed it for its black body, was an old Chevrolet with a single-long-front seat. Since I was the smallest of the three of us, I had been assigned the cramped space in the back, a makeshift seat that was not really a seat at all. But with my backpack on, moving was a miracle-level feat.

From the Lisa Frank collection, the backpack was my favorite. From afar it was unmistakable sporting a hot pink with royal blue décor, not the most discreet choice for this kind of operation. Its bulk, stuffed with merchandise, pressed awkwardly into my back, and with La Pandita's busted shocks, every bump reverberated straight through to my bones. Before I could even start whining about the growing pins and needles in my legs, my mom, almost telepathically, tried to comfort me with a bit of news.

"Don't worry, it's almost time for you to get off," she said.

We drove through several dusty streets, and from my low vantage point, all I could see were the hills of Altavista, a neighborhood with a distinctly third-world feel, perched along the *Río Bravo*, offering a panoramic view of the *Uniteds*. As soon as we passed *El Cigarro*, a cigarette-phallic-shaped monument at the roundabout near the *Rapiditos Bip Bip*[15], we lowered the music. The tension thickened.

When we were about to turn onto the road leading up the main hill, La Pandita's brakes let out a sudden-high-pitched screech. I slammed forward with what felt like 2 Gs of force, hitting the back of the single seat. A few seconds later, after regaining my senses, I noticed the flickering red and blue lights glowing in the distance.

"It's a checkpoint," my stepdad said. "You'll have to get out here, Jacqueline."

"You go up the hill, we'll meet you up there, at the house on the corner," he added.

"But what if I get lost?" I asked shakily.

"Look for Nacho. Now go, get out and don't talk to anyone!" he snapped, urgency in his voice.

"We love you!" my mom shouted, her eyes bloodshot and full of incoming tears.

In a rush, with my backpack strapped tight, I jumped out of the truck and onto the street. The weight on my back burned, knowing well that I was carrying illicit substances. The instructions sounded simple: "Go up, find Nacho's house, don't talk to anyone". But as I looked up at the steep hill, I lost my bearings, and those simple instructions transformed into a riddle. Go up, but how far? What color was Nacho's house? Who was Nacho? I started to sweat,

---

[15] One of the most iconic convenience stores in Juárez

not from the heat, but from utter fear. Fear of getting lost. Worse yet, fear of running into the police.

The hill was deceptive, the more I contemplated it, the longer it seemed to stretch. I gathered my courage and started the climb, focusing on each step forward, eyes fixed to the ground. Altavista was blanketed in hills, and most of its streets lacked luxuries like pavement or streetlights. If you were getting around on foot, it was common to own at least two pairs of sneakers (assuming you could afford them): one beat-up pair for trudging through the dirt roads, and another, decent pair reserved for everything else.

It is worth mentioning that I only had one pair, the all-purpose tennis shoes. So, as I fixed my gaze on the ground, I watched my sneakers slowly cake over with dust, as I listened to the crunch of countless pebbles shifting beneath each step I took. I had the vague but unmistakable feeling of being watched, maybe by the nosy old ladies hidden behind their window curtains, or maybe by the police, carrying out some kind of search-and-seize operation for little girl traffickers. Maybe both. The uncertainty of it all drilled through any coherent thought that stubbornly attempted to offer me comfort.

"There is no ill that lasts a hundred years," I remembered my mom's words, the ones she always murmured when we found ourselves in yet another pickle.

I cannot recall how long I kept climbing that hill, trapped in a trance of relentless anxiety, with my head down the entire way. But as I felt the darkness creep in and noticed my shadow beginning to fade,

I started to panic. Had I gotten lost? Certainly, this was absurd! How could something as simple as walking up a hill and finding a house turn into *Mission Impossible* (the Mexican edition)?

"I'm intelligent, I'm brave, I can do this. I'm intelligent, brave, I can do this. I'm intelligent, brave, I can do this," I repeated out loud, over and over, trying to convince myself that it was true.

With the last scraps of daylight, I began scanning the houses around me, studying each one carefully, imagining Nacho and his family coming and going through the decorative iron gates that framed their homes. A few interior lights started to flicker on, and I realized the night was catching up with me threatening to swallow whatever was left of my search. I thought about sitting down. The weight of the backpack, barely ten kilos, became unbearable. "Maybe if I sit, someone will find me," I told myself. But I quickly averted the thought. There did not seem to be any safe place to rest. And really, under these circumstances, with this backpack and my being alone, what place could be safe?

Even though I was just a child, I took pride in being courageous. Which is why I felt a surge of anger when I sensed the sting of traitorous tears rolling down the layer of dust that had settled on my cheeks. Holding back the choking sensation became inconceivable. The knot in my throat tightened, and I broke into a quiet sob. I did not want anyone to hear me, not the nosy old ladies, not the police out on a manhunt, not even the crickets. Maybe it was due to shame or the fear that someone would find me, alone, lost, and carrying an overstuffed Lisa Frank backpack.

In mid crisis, I perceived a sudden swirl of dirt rise into my nose, triggering the threat of a sneeze. Evidently, I was not alone, and now the proof was not just the vague feeling ruminating in my head. With the sleeve of my sweater, I wiped the stream of snot from my face, tightened the straps on my backpack, and braced myself to run. That is when I heard an unfamiliar voice, that of a young man. Not threatening but unsettling all the same.

"Hey, wait, it's okay. You're El Gemelo's daughter, right?" he asked.

I remained unresponsive.

"Look, we've all been looking for you. My name's Carlos. Come on, I'll take you to your parents," he insisted with a calm and steady tone.

With my nerves on edge and unable to trust him outright, I asked the first thing that came to mind, some kind of test to see if this Carlos really had been sent to find me or if he was just some *robaniñas*[16], and I was next on his list.

"Okay then, what is my stepdad wearing?"

"I don't know, white shorts and a black T-shirt. Now come on already!" he replied, his voice slipping into that impatient teenage tone.

White shorts and a black T-shirt.

White shorts and a black T-shirt.

---

[16] Kidnapper of little girls

White shorts and a black T-shirt.

I took a deep breath. My stepdad had been wearing light denim shorts and a navy-blue T-shirt. Nothing white, nothing black. Had this supposed Carlos simply mixed up the colors in the dim light? Or was it a setup? A trap? A storm of questions raced through my mind in a matter of seconds. I felt cornered, caught between the muzzle of a gun and the blade of a knife. My parents had told me not to speak to anyone. But they had also said it would be easy to find Nacho. After weighing every possibility and realizing that, one way or another, I was in boiling water, I resigned myself to trust the teenager, but with utter reticence.

"Alright, Carlos, I'll go with you. I'll follow, but take it slow, I'll stay behind you," I told him firmly.

"Suit yourself but hurry up. *La chota*[17] is out heavy around here, and if they stop us, I'm out and you'll have to figure it out on your own," he snapped back, bluntly and impatiently.

We walked for about five minutes, me clinging to my backpack like my life depended on it, and him pushing his bike, both of us moving through the night in an uncomfortable silence. Every instinct in me was lit up, firing on all cylinders. As we moved to the rhythm of the crickets, I kept scanning for an escape route, any viable way out in case I had monumentally fucked up.

By the time we reached the end of the block, under the only working streetlight in the whole neighborhood,

---

[17] Slang for the police

I finally caught sight of the chaotic scene ahead. Cars were blocking the street from all angles, parked every which way. People were moving around like ants from a freshly stomped anthill. It looked like the command center for a search-and-rescue mission as if they were out hunting for a lost girl with a backpack full of contraband.

Carlos turned around, flashed a sly, half-mocking grin, and said, "See? We were ALL out looking for you".

Just then, I heard my mother's hysterical cries. A few more tears betrayed me as I saw her running towards me. Turned out I had made the right call trusting Carlos. I slipped off the backpack and handed it over to the outstretched hand that suddenly appeared in front of me. Nacho. I had never seen him in my life, but he looked like he was the one in charge.

"You empty it out and bring it back, it's my favorite backpack," I demanded as I handed over the vivid hot pink and royal blue bundle.

Stunned to witness the guts of a scrawny little girl with coke-bottle glasses, Nacho smiled and nodded. Off in the distance, my stepdad let out a loud laugh.

"You've got some serious balls, Jacqueline, but damn, you're real *güey*[18] for getting yourself lost like that!" he shouted.

I focused my eyes, and sure enough, he was wearing light denim shorts and a navy-blue T-shirt.

---

[18] Mexican slang that refers to someone, with many different meanings and uses, in this case it loosely translates to "dumbass"

El asesinato de Chachito el Chivo

The Assassination of Chachito the Goat

It was not even June when the plan to head out to the ranch was conceived. A whole summer away from the city's ruckus while we figured out where we would live once the new school year started. We needed time and peace to recharge our mental batteries. The idea was that I leave first with my grandma Chuya and her husband, Don Felipe. Then, a few weeks later, my parents and siblings would join us. But, as was too often the case, we were flat broke and needed to scrape money to stock up on supplies for the three months we would be away. La Paloma, our busted old white clunker from the Stone Age, also needed a serious tune-up if it was going to survive the six-hour highway drive and God knows however many more hours over dirt roads. But we were going to make it, one way or another, even if we had to fly across the Chihuahuan desert in La Paloma. At least that is what we told ourselves to ease the nerves.

The three of us set out early one morning in Don Felipe's micro-truck, which was loaded to the brim with suitcases full of clothes, grocery bags, jugs of water, and a cage full of chickens. There was not enough room for all of us in the cabin, so I ended up riding in the back the entire trip making the chickens some company. The ranch was only a few hours southwest of Ciudad Juárez, but in a scrappy antique, with a will of iron, driven by an old man with *sangre de atole*[19], the journey easily doubled in length.

The first few hours on the road felt endless. For a significant stretch of the trip, the mix of wind, direct sun, and dust rocked me into a kind of heat-struck daze until I would pass out, only to be jolted awake by a sudden stop or sharp turn. Every now and then, during a break, my grandma Chuya would check on me to "see if I was still alive". She would tap on the back window of the cabin, never getting off once. With my scarecrow hair and sun-flushed face, I would mumble a groggy "sí". Don Felipe, being a *macho* was a tad more attentive, and would get down to grab water and give me a quick glance-over.

"Come on, help me get the tortillas out of the cooler," he ordered one of the times he got down.

"Careful, Don Felipe, you're about to step on my foot," I warned, seeing his boot come dangerously close to crushing my toes.

"So, you can lay some eggs, eh!" he shot back with the sharp humoristic wit of a seasoned cowboy.

Finally, our arrival at the ranch was spectacular, though without much of the spectacle. We were greeted by Manuel, the caretaker, the only person who lived on the ranch when my grandparents, or the owners, were not around. Manuel was a quiet and thin man, and years of the harsh desert sun had left his skin loose and weathered, like that of a

---

[19] An old way of saying someone is slow mannered

secondhand baseball glove. As soon as we pulled in, he helped unload the pile of junk from the truck, chickens and all. He was not much of a talker, and the only acknowledgment he gave me was a slight nod with one eyebrow raised. Not that I was a talker either. I preferred to take things in quietly. But being used to the city's chaos, I quickly realized there was not much to take in here, just a few animals and an endless stretch of desert.

The fenced-in area of the ranch stretched for what felt like miles, the kind of distance that looked like it might wrap around the whole world. Within the inhabited part of the land, there were only three houses: Manuel's, small and bare-bones; my grandparents', spacious, homey, painted a soft salmon; and the Fuentes', sterile and luxurious. Since the owners hardly ever came around, we used their house to shower but always with cold water, since the water heater stayed off when they were gone, and to stash the extra packs of *winnies*[20] and cartons of milk we had brought from Juárez. Out behind the Fuentes' house, there was a round fishbowl-shaped pool that had started to grow its own little aquatic ecosystem. Nearby were the horse stables, the chicken coop, and the granary.

Mr. Fuentes, knowing well my grandma Chuya's religious devotion, had also built her a small chapel on the west side of the compound. The white exterior was trimmed with a horizontal band in the typical

---

[20] Hot dogs in Juárez slang

Fuentes' color palette, bluish green and sunbaked earth tones. Inside, the chapel held two rows of three wooden pews and an altar adorned with a modestly sized painting of the *Virgen de Guadalupe*.

As the introverted child I was, I swiftly claimed the chapel as my own private and peaceful place. Back then, when I still clung tightly to my faith, I would pray with my grandma in the afternoons. I never managed to learn the full Our Father or the rosary, and because of that, my grandma would scold me for being "rebellious and a brat". So, she would leave me there as long as I needed, thinking I was practicing the prayers, hoping I would finally memorize them. What she did not know was that I used that solitude not for prayer, but to cool off from the afternoon heat and drift into imaginary places and scenes, in perfect tranquility.

I do not remember how long we were without my parents and my siblings; I just remember the day they arrived. La Paloma announced her entrance from afar leading a trail of dust that looked like the long and flowy veil of a bride. As they made their way, their fuss was distinguishable. From the distance I could clearly hear a hodge-podge of: Chalino crackling through a half-dead speaker, La Paloma's wheezing engine, and my mother's screams. But their commotion was immaterial. What mattered was that we were all together and I finally had my parents' protection against my grandma's militaristic regime.

"Ufff, amá, you should've seen La Paloma," my stepdad feverishly started to narrate. "All of a sudden, right after she'd been teetering for hours, she flew across the desert, almost revitalized. We were all bummed, thinking we weren't gonna make it, but then she pulls out some God-given strength and bam, we rolled up right to the gate. But I don't think she's gonna make it back..."

"Don't take the Lord's name in vain, *mijo*," my grandma interrupted flatly.

While I was unpacking the groceries from the *S-Mart* bags Don Felipe and Manuel had just unloaded from the trunk, my grandma turned to look at me and my brother.

"And you two, get out there and sweep the front!" she shouted.

Without thinking twice, Andrés and I, just a couple of four-and-eight-year-old-snot-nosed kids, leaned on the order as an excuse to bolt out of the house. We found the only two decent brooms and began sweeping the dirt off the sidewalk, a task that, looking back, feels counterintuitive on a ranch in the middle of the Chihuahuan desert. As we made our way around the house, not exactly in a hurry, we noticed El Guante, Don Felipe's brindle-colored dog, fast asleep, tied to the window railing.

"Why don't you go sweep over there, he won't bother you," Andrés urged me hesitantly.

"No, he's mean; I'm scared," I replied.

Thinking that what daunted me most was not the dog but my grandma, I swallowed hard, gathered my courage, and started gently sweeping around El Guante. Without noticing, his little eyes had opened, and his teeth, already bared, were beginning to gleam in a threatening snarl. In a flash, El Guante broke free from his chain and lunged at me, sinking his teeth into my waist with all the force of his ranch-raised jaws. My brother, frozen and unsure of what to do, grabbed his broom and tried to scare the dog off but only managed to redirect El Guante's fury. While I writhed in pain and shock, I heard my brother scream, "My knee! Help, help!" El Guante, a wild dog raised on the ranch, had sunk his teeth into my brother's leg before Don Felipe and Manuel managed to tear him off.

Consequently, during the three months we lived at my grandma's house, my brother and I kept our distance from El Guante, out of fear and respect. That said, not all my encounters with the ranch's fauna were hostile. Quite the opposite. I would spend hours watching the fish swim in the pond, and every now and then I would help Don Felipe and Manuel herd the cows on horseback. I used to ask Don Felipe how it was that the cows did not run off through the parts where there was no fence.

"Look, you see those metal bars on the ground? That's so the cows can't cross, if they try, their hooves get stuck," he explained one afternoon.

The image of a cow trapped for days under the sun felt cruel to me, but I was assured that never happened.

"Cows aren't stupid."

The ones you really had to keep an eye on were the goats. According to Manuel, those were some mischievous devils, some real *cabrones*. It was not uncommon for one to slip out of the pen and wander around bleating until someone hauled it back to its pen. I did not think that because they liked a little freedom, they were devils. In fact, I enjoyed watching them when no one else was around to rile them up. All they did was chew straw and bleat in unison.

One in particular had taken a liking to me. Whenever he saw me approaching the gate, Chachito, as I called him, would wander over to chew beside me. We would spend long bouts of time quietly focused on our own tasks: me sitting there playing with bits of straw, and him munching away at it. He let me feed him, and sometimes even allowed a few strokes on his head. My visits to the pen to see Chachito became part of the routine that kept me sane amid the long, dull stretches of ranch life.

One day, right near the end of our summer stay in that place so far removed from everything, the cowboys called me to the corral with urgency, without explaining the reason for all the commotion.

"Time for you to toughen up, Jacqueline, let this be a lesson," I heard someone say.

As I approached, I saw Manuel inside the corral with Chachito tied up by the legs. He turned as if to confirm I was watching and, with the kind of ease that only comes from practice, pulled a knife from his belt and, in one swift motion, slit my poor goat's throat. It all happened so rapidly that even as I stood there staring at Chachito sprawled across the straw, bleeding out, I could not quite process what had just happened. They had killed him, my Chachito, as some twisted plot to teach me a lesson.

Later that evening, Chachito appeared on my plate, chopped into pieces, served alongside a small mound of orange rice and refried beans. My grandma ordered me to eat everything. If I did not want what was on my plate, then I simply would not eat that night.

I left the table without saying a word, without so much as touching my plate, and headed to the only place I knew no one would come looking for me, the chapel. As I shut the door and caught the scent of the candle my grandmother always kept lit for the Virgin, I collapsed onto the floor and burst into tears. The image of Chachito, lifeless on the same straw where he used to let me feed him, kept ruminating in my mind. How could we be so cruel? Overwhelmed by helplessness, I grabbed the candle and hurled it against the wall. And so, at the age of eight, in front of the painting of the *Virgen de Guadalupe*, the only witness to my fit of rage, I decided to do two things right then and there: one, to become an atheist and two, a vegetarian.

I Don't Want to Die Alone

To begin this story, I must first confess that the remorse I feel as I write, despite all the years that have passed, is the same I felt when Doña María died. I was a little girl, a lonely one, when I met her. We had just moved in with my uncle, El Negro, after our failed year in the United States. He lived on one of the hills in Altavista, just behind the Pemex gas station. In that neighborhood, the warning "aguas"[21] came to life, literally, when the sewage surged and mixed with the torrential rains that regularly flooded the streets. Since the roads were not paved, we would then have to wade through a stew of diluted human excrement and mud just to leave or return home.

In truth, we did not really have much reason to brave out the sludge anyway. There was not much to do or a dime to prompt any outings. My uncle was the only one who, religiously, whether under riddling rain or the scorching sun, made his daily trek to the corner store, the *Rapiditos Bip Bip*, for his much-needed fix, a family-sized-*caguama*[22]. All that effort to keep faithful to his vigorously inebriated liver.

---

[21] Literately translating to "waters" is a word used all over Mexico to forewarn someone of trouble ahead
[22] A large-one-liter beer bottle

A few months before we went to live with him, his son Samy, a seven-year-old kiddo, had been killed. One ordinary afternoon, as he was walking home from school, a freight truck ran him over. The driver had been drinking. When it came time to account for what happened, the witnesses told my aunt Eva, almost with morbid fascination, that they saw her son's brains erupt like shrapnel as his head burst open under the wheel. I never understood why that detail was necessary.

I must admit that when we got the news, I experienced insatiable blame. It had not been long since I had last seen Samy, and the last I did before we said goodbye was grab his hand and force him into a "reading". Because I had been giddily practicing my witch abilities, everyone who crossed my path was subjected to an involuntary palm analysis.

"Look, this is your love line, and if you close your hand, right here are the children," I told him. "Looks like you're not going to have any kids."

"Good! I don't want any!" he snapped back.

"Here's your lifeline. Samy, this says you're going to die really soon."

We snickered at that psychic revelation and went on with our baseball game. A few weeks later, Samy was crushed by a freight truck. The driver was drunk. I never read another palm again.

Later, a trial was held, and my aunt and uncle were awarded a modest sum as compensation for Samy's death. With that, they bought a humble plot of land in Altavista and built their home, a single large room that quartered both the kitchen and the beds in one space. But the money only stretched far enough to put up the walls and install a wooden roof. The floor, made of hardened dirt, was compacted through regular hosing, while the bare, unplastered walls stood exposed, revealing the rough gray of the concrete blocks. Toward the end, the bathroom was sectioned off by walls that did not quite reach the ceiling, and a curtain, draped over the entrance in place of a door. I do not remember there being any running water inside, only the outdoor *pila*, the same one used to hose the dirt floor.

That is where we landed: five of us crammed together after a short-lived *gringo* stint that ended abruptly with my stepdad's inevitable deportation. Midway through the school year in the *Uniteds*, my stepdad got locked up after they found a minuscule bag of cocaine in his jeans' pocket. Once they realized he did not have papers, ICE sent him to a detention center to be shipped off to Ciudad Juárez. We had no choice but to leave El Paso and follow him, all of us with our tails between our legs and not a *peso* to our name, not even a place to drop dead.

In that moment my aunt and uncle took us in, offering shelter in their humble home, where the five of us squeezed into a full-size bed under a single tiger-print blanket, curled up right next to my uncle's bed. That is where the tragic story of Doña María and her two tanks of gas began.

Like I mentioned before, we showed up at my uncle's place halfway through the school year, unable to finish my classes. Those months we lived in Altavista I spent completely *desquehacerada*[23]. After one failed run-in with the neighborhood kids, my mom banned me from making friends with those "vandals who only knew how to steal". I accepted my role as a lonely kid, bored and without the busyness of schoolwork, with complete resignation.

My chores, and only source of entertainment, were hauling water, looking after the animals, and running errands to the *S-Mart*, which was a good half-hour walk away. One time, as I was walking back from the grocery store and climbing up the hill, I saw our neighbor, an old woman with her hair tied back, bent over in her yard picking at the ground. She looked like a hen pecking at corn, except she was gathering tree branches and sticks off the dirt.

"Doña María, what are you doing? Let me help you," I offered, seeing her so focused on that strange task.

"Ah, *mija*, yes, look, I'm searching for wood scraps to put in my heater. It's real cold," she replied, one hand on her hip, never breaking her hen-like rhythm.

For the proceeding hours, we combed through her whole yard for any tree scraps that could serve as firewood. While I bent down to gather twigs and

---

[23] A way of saying "with nothing to do"

she held open the plastic bag, Doña María told me about her life in the city. At age ninety, she had lived through experiences I could not even fathom at ten. She lived alone because her husband had passed away two years earlier. Her only inheritance was two adult children, her humble two-room house, and two gas tanks, each a meter and a half tall.

"He and I couldn't stand each other by the end. Fernando was already half bitter, and I just pretended not to hear him most of the time," she said.

"But I miss him," she added. "Now I don't even have anyone to argue with."

Her children, as far as inheritance went, were not of much value either. If it was not neglect, it was abuse. Her eldest daughter lived in El Paso and came once a month in her maroon van to drop off supplies. As soon as she unloaded the four grocery bags from Walmart onto the kitchen table, she would hop back in her van and speed off. Her son, on the other hand, was nothing but a first-rate junkie who took advantage of her vulnerability, robbing her of what little she had left just to get high in the backyard. Doña María was terrified of him. She told me that when he was "using", he would beat her.

"I yell for help, but no one comes."

During those months of my *desquehaceramiento*, I tried to keep her company. There was not a single afternoon I did not spend at least an hour sitting with her on her front porch, both of us perched on her old, half-rotted wooden bench. Seeing how committed I was, my mom started setting aside dinner portions for me to take to her, knowing how hard it was for the old woman to cook since her stove ran on gas. When her husband died, he left her two full gas tanks. But even with militaristic rationing, she ran out within the first year. For the year that followed, the tanks stayed chained to the window grate, collecting cobwebs. As we sat on the porch, Doña María would regularly tell me her dream was to get those tanks refilled. At night, she was scared to leave the firewood burning in the heater.

"I don't want to die alone and burned in my bed," she confessed.

I made her dream my secret mission. I had an uncle who rented out rooms to migrants from Veracruz who, back in the '90s, had come to Juárez in waves. If anyone could render aid for Doña María, it was him. But my uncle was never around when we went looking for him. The one time we did catch him, he half-listened and suggested I just buy her new tanks, since refilling them was tricky because the gas trucks did not drive "in those parts".

"Well then, go buy some new ones, but they're expensive, eh. Don't count on me, I'm not out here handing out charity."

Hearing his dismissive, almost mocking tone, I felt completely defeated. I knew my uncle was not the most generous soul, evidenced particularly in the manner in which he exploited migrants for his own economic gain. But now what? I did not have the money to buy two new gas tanks; I could barely scrape together enough pesos for the *rutera* we took back and forth. Winter was starting to creep in, and I could not imagine how many blankets Doña María would need just to get through the night. We had already used up all the tree scraps in her yard, and it was nearly impossible to find any more wood to burn. Gradually and with increasing disappointment, I began to let go of the mission. It became harder, almost nuisance-like, to listen to her complain about the cold. I started visiting her less, and when I did, just seeing the tanks, covered in cobwebs, irritated me.

"You don't visit me as much anymore. I don't know if maybe you're upset with me?" she asked one time.

"No, Doña María, it's just that I've been really busy lately," I lied, avoiding her gaze.

Lying to the old woman felt inherently odd. Why had I not spoken honestly? Why not say I was ashamed for failing the mission? As I tortured myself with questions, the quiet hum of a white car creeping up the hill interrupted my internal deliberation. The Avon lady was coming to drop off last month's orders. Eager by the unfolding scene, knowing that inside those bags there were a lip balm and some perfumed lotions with my name on them, I jumped off the bench like a spring and rushed to say goodbye to Doña María. She asked when I would visit her again, to which I half-mumbled as I was running out, "I don't know, I don't know!" without looking back.

The days passed and turned into weeks. Amid the commotion of a possible move, I forgot, or perhaps avoided, to pay my little old lady a visit. It was easy to forget her; those days, she was seen less and less. Eventually, she stopped being seen altogether.

One morning, just before the alarm went off, my mother wrestled me awake, exclaiming that something was happening on the block. Frightened and shivering with cold, I threw off the blankets and rushed to the window. The slope just in front of Doña María's house was teeming with people. Some were crying, others trying to instill order in the chaos, but most were just spectators. When I saw Doña María's door wide open, a knot twisted tightly in my stomach. I pulled away from the window with a sensation somewhere between nausea and suffocation. The adults had already rushed ahead to crowd into the chaos and play detective. I ran barefoot out of the house, slipping through the gaps in the wall of people huddled in front of Doña María's yard, the same yard we had cleared of sticks.

I finally emerged from the sea of people, just at edge of the porch, next to the two tanks of gas chained up against the window. I took a deep breath, bracing myself for what I was about to see. When I stepped inside the house, I saw her. Doña María was lying on her bed beneath two blankets, one a faded purple flannel, the other handmade with a floral pattern stitched into its fabric. Her bare arms gently cradled her body atop the woven flowers. Her face, wrinkled just as I remembered, had lost its warm cinnamon hue, replaced by a pale chestnut tone. But what struck me most was seeing her eyes shut. The old woman had died in her sleep.

I did not cry and have not since. Remorse was the only thing I felt when I saw her lying under her two blankets. I abandoned her because I did not know how to cope with my own incompetence in the face of her misery. She was my friend, and I traded her for an Avon order. I left her hanging on the eve of my visit, which I never again made until that moment.

It seems that her daughter from El Paso, under the threat of winter, took pity on her and managed to get her a small gas tank. Doña María died of asphyxiation, poisoned by carbon monoxide, while she slept. Alone, but at least not burned.

Sometimes I think her insistence on getting her gas tanks filled was not so much about the cold, but because having gas made her feel less alone, like when her husband was still alive. The truth is I do not know. These are the things I tell myself to soothe my guilt. But maybe that thought only digs in the knife of guilt into my heart just a bit deeper.

LAS PENAS CON PAN
(Y UNA COCA DE A LITRO)

Sorrows with Bread
(and a Liter of Coke)

Every time it rained, the inner streets of Waterfill Avenue would flood. The lack of pavement turned everything into a mud pit for two days, until the desert's persistent drought would harden the dirt into a kind of makeshift concrete. For residents of La Satélite neighborhood, navigating the rain had become an Olympic sport. If they were privileged enough to own a car, their tires would get stuck in the mud and spin helplessly, leaving them with two options: wait out the two days or assemble an improvised team of neighbors to push and free the car from the mire. Those traveling on foot had to either invest in rubber boots or risk ruining their only pair of shoes just to wade through the muck and reach Waterfill on their way to the bus stop.

My house, a modest-sized two-room space with a concrete floor, sat right in the middle of all that mess. Fortunately, we rarely went out, since during the time we lived there, I was skipping school. We moved to La Satélite after spending a few months crashing with my uncle El Negro.

This was one of the most challenging times during our years in Juárez. My stepfather had been deported from the United States, and my mother, my siblings, and I had fled back to Juárez for safety reasons. Since we had nowhere to live, my uncle generously offered us a shared space in his home until we were able to find a little shack for the five of us.

"Jacqueline, always remember that a dead person and a houseguest start to stink after three days," my mother used to say.

We moved in August, right at the start of what should have been my fifth grade. But school was a touchy subject we avoided, because my mother was ashamed that she could not afford the luxury of sending us. Instead, we focused on the present day and on the household chores, which were not too demanding since cleaning two rooms did not take long. However, what caused a whole marathon of trouble was not having a proper water source or drainage on-site. To bathe, wash clothes, rinse dishes, and cook, we stole water from the vacant lot across the street, which, miraculously, had a water faucet liberally exposed.

Every morning, my two younger siblings and I would sneak out *despichaditamente*[24] into the lot across the street, under strict orders from my mother that "nobody better see us" carrying three empty buckets. In a matter of minutes, those that stretched long under the threat of getting caught, we would fill the buckets with water and run back to the house, triumphant.

---

[24] A word used largely in the northern part of Mexico meaning "stealthily"

Since the house was not equipped with a drainage system either, the other challenging task was using the restroom. We did not have a porcelain toilet. We mounted a toilet seat with a lid on top of a green bucket and voilà, we turned that improvisation into a wobbly throne. But we faced two problems: one, having to keep our balance on the seat so as not to fall off and, in turn, not splatter our digestion into an artistic mess all over the floor and wall; and two, having to haul our waste immediately after each use to the empty lot across the street, the same one we stole water from. That last problem was the most humiliating. I would hold it until nighttime to relieve myself, knowing that under the cover of darkness there was a lower incidence of getting caught in mid-shitty mission.

Getting bored was also part of the routine because, despite the daily battles with hauling water and using the restroom, there was not much else to do. The television, which only picked up two channels, the one with *Sábado Gigante* and the other with the afternoon telenovelas, broke down regularly. The only reading material I had were four school textbooks in English that my aunt from El Paso had given us, "so the girl does not fall too far behind in school".

Every morning, before carrying out the water chores, while the others were fast asleep, I would sneak out to the backyard and sit cross-legged, with my four textbooks spread out on the ground. I reread all the lessons, longing for school. I liked the images that showed classrooms with whiteboards carpeted with printed cardboard decorations. During those placid mornings, I would teleport myself to another life, that of a girl in a school uniform sitting at a desk with my Scribe notebook and a colorful set of gel pens, learning about world geography and Greek mythology.

There were days when that imaginary trip stretched out. My parents, always in search of work, would regularly head out with my siblings. They would leave me behind alone because the *rutera* cost a *chingo*[25], and I was big enough to look after myself. By staying home, they saved fourteen pesos, seven to head out and seven to return. I did not complain; we barely had enough to buy a liter of milk, so that bit of savings came in handy. And so, during those prolonged absences, I would simply travel through time and space with my four textbooks, not knowing when my family would return.

On New Year's Day, my parents departed with the hope of gathering some cash so that we could feast with tacos de *tripitas* from the corner shop. Once again, I was left alone, holding on to the idea that that night we would celebrate in delicious fashion. The hours elapsed one after another, and I stayed cut off from the world with no word from my family as the night fell. The anxiety of not knowing where they were or whether they were coming back ate me alive. I no longer cared about the tacos. When the clock

---

[25] Colloquial way of saying "a lot"

struck eleven, I decided to turn on the television to distract myself with the New Year's Eve celebrations.

I remember counting down the twelve seconds in unison with Don Francisco from *Sábado Gigante*, imagining a bowl full of grapes, and closed my eyes to welcome the new year. We officially welcomed the year 2000. That night I cried because I did not know if I would ever see my family again. I wrote a letter to my mom telling her how much I loved her. My tears had smudged the ink on some of the words. I folded it and placed it neatly on the kitchen table. Finally, I went to sleep without knowing if I would wake up. As we headed into a new century, rumors circulated that 2000 was the year of God and that all sinners would die, only those who were free of sin would be protected in a bubble from the wrath that would be unleashed. Was I a sinner? Were my parents?

When I woke up the following morning, I made two immediate observations. One, I clearly was not a sinner, and two, everyone was sound asleep in their respective beds. In the kitchen, I saw my letter spread out on the table, open, next to a brown paper bag full of sweet bread. I pulled out the little pig-shaped one, which gave off a soft aroma of anise, and snuck out to the backyard to imagine myself somewhere else, but with my family still whole.

It is well known that after the holidays, everyone is irrevocably broke. As much as my parents tried to find money during their long absences, they always came back home defeated. The sweet bread would be eaten stale, while the tortillas, now hardened, were only good for cutting into square pieces and mixing with eggs. But there were times when we could not even afford stale bread, or tough tortillas, or eggs. In her desperation, my mom would send me to the *abarrotería*[26] on the corner to ask for *fiado*[27]. I felt deeply embarrassed every time I stepped inside, always with my head down, because the owner, Mrs. Rosales, standing behind her glass counter, would yell at me the moment she saw me enter.

"Uff no, here you come begging again! I already told your mother not to send you until she pays everything that she owes me!"

I would walk back home crying, humiliated, and hungry.

One time, while my brother and I were exploring the abandoned lots in the neighborhood, we came up with the idea of collecting cans and scrap metal to sell at the scrapyard on Waterfill. Back then, the metal went for two pesos a kilo. If we could gather ten kilos, we could walk past Mrs. Rosales' store without having to ask for credit.

Thrilled by the math, we began scouring every street in La Satélite in search of scrap. The peak winter weather allowed for long shifts without the

---

[26] Small mom and pop shops in lower income neighborhoods that sell snacks, drinks, and some basic grocery items all paid in cash
[27] Translates to asking for "credit" which were typical and oftentimes informal arrangements in smaller mom and pop stores; shop owners would pull out a notebook and handwrite the debts to keep record

necessity to stop and rest as frequently. But despite the hours walked and kilometers covered, our plastic bag barely reached four kilos. The neighborhood had already been picked clean. We sat down, nearly defeated, when my brother smiled, one of those sly, mischievous grins.

"And what if we fill the cans with sand?!" he exclaimed.

It was an undeniably devious but promising idea. With no better option, I nodded, and we immersed ourselves in the delicate task of packing each can with a handful of sand. We must have looked like just two lonely kids in the middle of a vacant lot, innocently playing with dirt and trash.

When we arrived at the scrapyard, completely covered in grime, we began to sweat as we waited in line behind the other sellers. Most of them were older men in cowboy hats, faded-saggy pants from overuse, and cinnamon-colored hands encroached by arthritis. When our turn came, my brother handed the plastic bag to the woman behind the scale. As she read the number the scale displayed, she looked up and smiled, realizing these two little brats were trying to pull a fast one on her.

"Nine kilos," she announced.

She winked at us in complicity and handed over eighteen pesos. We had managed to hack the system, doubling the weight of our cans with nothing but trickery, and now we had something to surprise our mother with when we got home. We ran to Mrs.

Rosales's store, and just as she began to frown and prepared to shoo me away, I slammed the eighteen pesos onto the counter with victorious force.

"Give us four *bolillos*[28], a quarter kilo of ham, one avocado, and a liter of Coke, please," I demanded confidently.

On the way home, I remembered the saying "sorrows with bread taste better", and figured that with ham, avocado, and an iced-cold Coke, our sorrows might just taste like glory.

Beware of the
Greek God Perverts

On the corner lived a woman in her fifties with an air of Doña Florinda[29], who used to travel with her two daughters once a month. No one ever saw her daughters, we only noticed her absence because the kitchen window facing the interior courtyard of our enclosed community would remain shut while she was away. We had nicknamed her Mrs. Margarita[30], not because that was her name, but because her bitterness was evidenced in the way she would slam the broom against the sidewalk as she swept in front of her house. She never listened to the radio, never danced, never chatted with the other neighbors. Mrs. Margarita belonged to another social class, and we were her neighborhood's riffraff, giving her well-deserved daily baths of *pueblo* grime in icy bucketfuls.

"Get out of the way, you little vandals!" she would shout at us with disdain every time she was sweeping and ran into one of us.

Her husband, on the other hand, like most men who have resigned themselves to the relentless, overbearing buzz of feminine reproach, kept himself locked up inside their modest home. He only came out for two reasons: to light the water heater out back, and

---

[29] Character in the famous Mexican series, *El Chavo del Ocho*
[30] Margarita is a play on words with the word *amargada* which translates to a "bitter woman"

to smoke a knockoff Marlboro in silence. When Mrs. Margarita traveled, during those stretches of the shut window, the only sign of life in that house was the faint sound of Marco Antonio Solís singing, "I miss you more than ever and I don't know what to do".

Aside from the house on the corner, there were four other humble dwellings clustered within our enclosed community. Upon entering the courtyard, Mrs. Margarita's home stood to the right, and to the left, a row of three modest apartments and a rear house. These four households shared a single bathroom, a windowless cave with a concrete floor and walls painted a murky seaweed green. The only light inside came from a bare bulb hanging from the ceiling by a wire, which swayed threateningly each time the steel door was slammed shut, as if always on the verge of shattering against the wall.

Each of the four families, excluding the one in the corner house, took part in daily chores and helped care for the children. One of the shared tasks was doing the laundry. My mom had bought a washing machine that everyone used, and whenever we took our turn with it, the others helped hang the clothes to dry.

During sluggishly hot evenings, the other kids and I would gather in one of the four homes to play *lotería*. We placed modest bets, ten pesos at most, which, if we were lucky enough to shout, "¡Lotería!", we would spend at the *fondita*[31] on the corner, where burritos cost only five pesos.

I had become particularly friendly with one of my neighbors, Karen, a Black girl my age. Her family, originally from southern Mexico, was the first Black family I had ever met in Ciudad Juárez. At the time, a wave of migration from different parts of the country had begun to slowly unravel the once-homogeneous seams of our border city.

"Where are you from?" I asked the first time I saw her.

"We came from Oaxaca, supposedly just to cross the border, but we ended up staying here," she replied.

"Is Oaxaca pretty?" I asked. "Juárez is a real dusty mess, I'm sorry you are here."

"Yeah, it's pretty, but I like the sunsets here more. The sky turns pink and orange," she said with a genuine look in her eyes.

That was how Karen and I became inseparable friends, thick as thieves. She was a sharp, quick-witted girl who never missed a beat. Whenever we played *bebeleche*[32], Karen kept a close eye on my every move, making sure I always landed squarely within the lines. If I wobbled even a little and my shoe grazed the chalk, she would sound the alarm and gleefully declare it her turn.

---

[31] Small and modest restaurants that sell home style meals for affordable prices, generally in lower income neighborhoods
[32] The game of hopscotch

I, on the other hand, was less, let us say, competitive. I often drifted off into the clouds, distracted by the miniscule happenings of our block. Once, for example, I became fixated on a zoomorphic scene unfolding near the openings in the wall outside the bathroom. For hours, I watched intently as a spider had tangled up an ant and stood guard, waiting for the perfect moment to feast on its banquet. After such a long, anticlimactic wait, I picked up a thin stick and unraveled the ant from its torture. When the spider saw its prey slip away, it went wild, cursing me out, in what I imagine was arachnid.

Karen and I used to sit on the curb that bordered the front of the apartments, delighting in the breezy summer nights. With our legs dangling over the edge, we would sip on strawberry-flavored Fanta poured into clear plastic bags, each with a straw tied off with a rubber band, like two little old ladies gossiping over coffee. The conversation was the usual: "What do you want to be when you grow up?", "Which boy on the block do you like the most?", "Which one do you like the least?"

Every now and then, we engaged in much more serious conversations, but always with care. Karen would tell me how her stepfather beat her mom, and how she would run off to hide. That was why she spent so much time outside, like an untamed goat. I, in turn, would tell her about the times the teenage boys in the neighborhood had forced their hands down my pants under the excuse that we were playing some kind of rated-R version of truth or dare. After that confessional purge, we would hug, our eyes glassy, and start singing: "que llueva, que llueva, la virgen de la cueva..."

One night, during a closed-window spell, our block had been left without adults. In the dark, you could still make out the incandescent yellow glow shining from Mrs. Margarita's windows. Under that glow, Karen and I were enjoying our sodas when we heard the screech of the front door, followed by the soft thud of it closing. Startled by the sudden break in silence, we set out to investigate the suspicious scene. Who could be sneaking around the block so discreetly?

We figured the neighbor had gone out to light the water heater, but like two skeptics, we refused to trust our instincts without doing a bit of detective work first. Light on our feet like cats, with our index fingers pressed to our lips, we crept cautiously toward the entrance of Mrs. Margarita's abode. Sure enough, someone had just stepped out, because a sharp sliver of mustard-colored light was cutting through the doorway. The second door, the wooden one, had been left slightly ajar.

As we rounded the corner toward the boiler, we came upon the strange sight of the neighbor, Mrs. Margarita's husband. He wore an odd expression: a mischievous smile curled beneath his bare upper lip complemented by a set of flushed cheeks. But it was not his ambiguous face that sent shivers down our spines, but his nighttime attire. Instead of the usual shorts and t-shirt, he was modeling a white bedsheet wrapped under his armpits like a dress. He looked like a Greek god, but with the unmistakable twist of an inebriated, potbellied Mexican man.

At the sight of us, he did not showcase any evident surprise, it was as if he had been waiting for us. He looked at me and asked if I would like to go with him to his house so he could show me "something". I had not yet grasped the strangeness of the moment, and I felt drawn in by my deeply ingrained need to "listen to adults" and "be a good girl". Driven by the curiosity of that "something", I began to take a step forward when suddenly the neighbor dropped his Greek god bedsheet to the compacted dirt floor of the backyard. In a matter of seconds, I was faced with the pornographic image of a sagging body: two thin, wrinkled legs, a protruding belly casting a shadow over a stiff, upright member, and two hairy, drooping sacks beneath it.

Just when I was frozen in place, I felt Karen's frosty and firm hand grab mine hurriedly. My trance ruptured at the sound of her urgent plea: "Jacqueline, come on, quick, come!" We managed to get into my apartment. Karen quickly locked all the doors and windows. Frightened and short of breath, she hugged me and asked if I was okay. Still in shock, I told her yes but that I did not understand what was happening.

"Jacqueline, do you remember the boys from the neighborhood who make you play truth or dare?

Well, he was going to do the same thing, but worse," she told me.

That night, we cried together. We unbosomed, narrated the story repeatedly, laughed, shook with fear, cried some more. But what happened after that, I do not remember clearly.

Upon our parents' return, Karen relayed what had occurred, and they nearly lynched the neighbor on the spot. A few weeks later, we moved. I never knew if we left because my mom no longer felt safe in that neighborhood, or because we could no longer afford the rent. Either way. I also do not know what would have happened to me that night if Karen had not pulled me out of my trance of childish naivety. What I do know is that Karen was the first best friend I ever had, and one I never saw again.

LA JUARENITA
"AMERICANSER"

Juareñita 'Americanser'

The alarm clock was one of those with a radio option. Monday through Friday, the speaker of the tiny but powerful device would go haywire the moment three blinking red numbers announced 4:00 a.m. I never knew which intruder would slip into my dreams between songs each morning. Sometimes I woke to the booming voice of Vicente Fernández going on about beautiful women, and other times to an accordion-heavy tune by Ramón Ayala. What never failed, however, was my mother's groggy scream from under the covers during the impromptu concert.

"Jacqueline, wake up, come on, get ready!"

The intrusive music and my mother's weary voice were enough to frighten any lingering traces of sleep. With reluctant laziness and eye boogers blurring my sight, I would leave the warmth of my blankets and tiptoe, shivering toward the kitchen to light the stove with a match. On the burner, I would place a blue enamel pot filled with water and let it come to a boil. In the meantime, I would go to the bathroom to fetch the bucket from the shower. Once the water boiled, I poured it into the bucket and carried it back to the bathroom. I would fill the rest with lukewarm water and undress.

Bathing *a jicarazos*[33] in the middle of the desert winter felt like getting zapped with a jolt of icy electricity, only useful to reactivate all five senses at once. After those daily polar shocks, it was time for a second lotion bath, getting dressed, and tying my hair into a ponytail with a marble-bead elastic. All while I waited for my mother to get ready alongside my brother, who would throw half-asleep tantrums. The first part of "Operation School" was complete, and now it was time to embark on the second: traveling across the city in the *rutera* and crossing the international bridge by foot.

Every morning around five, my mother, brother, and I would leave the house like three bandits sheltered by the darkness, holding hands. Bundled up to our necks, the biting air stabbed straight through to our bones. By the time we made it down the hill and reached the bus stop, we were already covered in dust.

Once we were finally aboard the bus headed toward the Santa Fe bridge, I would watch in awe as the city slowly woke with the sunrise. At that ungodly hour, the only sounds were the sharp clang of metal shutters on the few early-opening shops and the low hum of the occasional car. Despite the exhaustion, I liked taking in the fleeting calm of the city before arriving at the booming chaos of downtown.

---

[33] In the absence of a traditional shower or bathtub, bathing that involves using a bucket filled with water and a small bowl to pour it over one's body

To signal our stop, we would shout "¡bajan!" to the bus driver, but not a sleepy, polite *bajan*[34], rather one shouted with soul, with anger, with urgency. Only then would the driver take notice. Upon the screeching stop, we would rapidly jump off through the back door of the bus, straight into the middle of a busy street, with the sole mission of avoiding getting run over by the oncoming swarm of vehicles.

The bus stop left us about a kilometer from the international bridge on foot. This part of our daily journey was my favorite because the street vendors would stir my hunger with the alluring smells of freshly cooked corn and churros bubbling in hot oil. With my stomach begging loudly for some greasy treat, I would tug at my mother's coat to signal my morning craving. As a good *juarense*, my mom would always order us burritos filled with *chile colorado* and beans, paired with thick *champurrados*. She would get herself a lukewarm Nescafé served in a white foam cup from one of the many orange coolers that flanked the food stands.

"When you are older, I will buy you a coffee, but for now, you just have to hold on," my mom would say as she caught me eyeing her little white cup with envy.

Even at a young age, the lack of caffeine was beginning to show in the many recurring mishaps I had during our trips. One time, just before I was

---

[34] Loosely translating to "getting off."

about to pay my five pesos to cross the bridge, I hit my chest against a telephone booth. Groggy and with my head down, I had a disastrous habit of staring at the ground instead of watching where I was going. Following the rushed, marathon-like pace of my mother, who was practically dragging me along for a few meters, I failed to notice that right in front of us, planted on the sidewalk, stood a telephone booth. Without warning, my chest slammed violently into the monument of the Telmex empire.

Upon hearing the abrupt thump that interrupted the usual hum of our morning trek, my mother came to a halt, and in sync with my scream, turned around to see what had caused the commotion. But instead of comforting me like a loving woman might, when she saw the scene, her whiny, half-asleep, nearsighted daughter sprawled out on the pavement, she burst into a sort of cruel chuckle.

"Ay, *mija*, you really are blind as a bat."

My clinical blindness was not limited to run-ins with telephone booths smack in the middle of the sidewalk, it extended to a wide range of unforeseen obstacles: uneven sidewalks, plantless planters, potholes, short poles, tall poles, medium poles, plastic bags filled with trash, bags of merchandise, just… bags.

But one of my most memorably tragic accidents had nothing to do with my blindness, rather with the loss of my *champurrado*. Halfway across the bridge, right at the entrance to the immigration hall, I slammed into one of the flaps of the plastic curtain shielding the interior from the cutting wind. I, distraught (as usual) and distracted (as usual), did not realize that when you push through the flaps of a curtain, under the laws of physics they must also come down. As the strip of curtain came back down with full force, my warm-thick *champurrado* crashed into my chest, splattering my jacket with a beige mess. I cried instantly, not because it hurt, but because it broke my heart that my mother's effort had ended up smeared across my clothes, face, and hair.

"Calm down, you can clean yourself up once we cross," my mother consoled me, half amused.

With no choice but to face my embarrassing misfortune, I stepped up to the glass booth where the immigration officer waited, ready to present both my American ID and whatever dignity I had left.

"Americanser[35]," I declared before he could ask why I smelled like cinnamon and toasted cornmeal.

Once we passed through immigration into Gringoland, we were greeted by El Paso's downtown. The contrast between two cities, two countries, was

---

[35] In the 1990s, it was typical to cross the international bridge by only saying "American, sir" to signal citizenship without showing any kind of proof; since I did not speak English, *Americanser* was my Spanish equivalent to "American, sir"

clearly exhibited in their downtowns. In Juárez, the racket seemed to carpet the blackened streets, petrified by years of grease and built-up grime. In El Paso, the shops remained gated at that morning hour. The calm on the American side was so profound that even the trembling of the wind could be heard. The sidewalks, too, enjoyed routine care. It was common to see men in orange jumpsuits hosing down the streets with an anaconda-style pressure hose. I would ask my mom if they used soap, and she would answer no, that the pressure alone was enough to "wash away all the filth".

"Why do they not use those hoses to clean the streets in Juárez, *mamá*?" I would also ask her.

"Oh, *mija*," she would answer with a smile.

It never became clear how many blocks we walked before catching the first bus. I just remember that, after passing the shoe store, *El Peiles*[36], the bus stop appeared just around the corner, covered in glass and lined with signs displaying all its schedules. This phenomenon fascinated me because in Juárez, the bus arrived when it arrived, and there was no way of knowing whether we would wait five minutes or an hour. The longest we ever had to wait for the bus in El Paso was twenty minutes, which I would use quietly to feed my Tamagotchi.

The ride once on the bus was different from the ones in Juárez. The roads were wider and much less

---

[36] Payless

congested. I also felt embarrassed having to board the bus and interact with the driver in English. Back then, my English was limited to "Americanser," the numbers, and "please" and "thank you". At least to get off, there was no need to shout "bajan", one had to simply press a yellow button or pull a cord that hung above the window.

Despite the extensive journey, which consisted of trekking down a hill, hopping on a *rutera*, walking a kilometer, crossing an international bridge, announcing "American, sir" to the customs officer, walking several more blocks, and taking two buses, we still had to walk another mile through the open desert to reach the school. After several hours in transit, the trip, without the lively street hustle of the sellers and food stalls in Juárez, became, let us say, a bit dull. So, to keep us entertained, my mom would have us practice the only three tongue twisters she knew.

First, we would start with the king.

"The king of Parangaricutirimícuaro wants to de-Parangaricutirimícuar himself. Whoever manages to de-Parangaricutirimícuar him will be a great de-Parangaricutirimícuar-er."

Then we would proceed with the one about taste.

"If my liking does not like what your liking likes, what a dislike it would be to find out that your liking does not like what my liking likes."

"In the countryside, there is an ética, perlética, pelambrética, peluda, pelapelambruda goat. She has éticos, perléticos, pelambréticos, peludos, pelapelambrudos baby goats. If the goat were not ética, perlética, pelambrética, peluda, pelapelambruda, she would not have had éticos, perléticos, pelambréticos, peludos, pelapelambrudos baby goats."

Finally, after so much tongue twisting about hairy goat talks, around 8:15 a.m., we would arrive at the entrance of my school, Loma Terrace Elementary. The image of the school mascot, a cartoonish lion, greeted us as we stepped into the main hallway. Right beneath the lion is where I had to say goodbye to my mother, a goodbye that caused me emotional turmoil. Without her maternal protection, it was just me against the other kids.

I am not exaggerating when I say "against" because for several years, at least the ones I spent crossing international borders to attend school, the bullying I endured was routine. For starters, I did not speak English, and when I tried, the girls would mock me: "Ken ay gou tu da restrum, plis?" The words I especially stumbled over were the ones that had "r" and "l" together, like "girl" and "world". At all costs, I avoided those because of the predictable ridicule that followed each one of my embarrassing pronunciations. But my reluctance around "rl" shifted around the middle of second grade, when I experienced my first childhood crush: a boy with glasses named Marco. Because he was clever and had a "global" mind, our teacher, Mr. Martínez, nicknamed him "World", to my great misfortune. So, if I wanted to interact with Marco, I had to learn to pronounce that complicated word.

It is worth mentioning that during those elementary school years, no topic was off-limits when it came to mockery. In addition to my English, my condemned pupils delighted in making fun of my appearance and my food. Because I wore thick glasses, they called me "four eyes" to which I would reply, "four eyes see better than two" even though that was not true, but it was enough to silence their attacks.

Lunchtime was the worst. While the other kids laid out their ham and singles' cheese sandwiches made with store-bought white bread and their Capri-Suns, I pulled out the *chile colorado* burrito my mom had bought me on the way to the bridge. As soon as I set it down on the table, the contrast between my lunch and everyone else's was striking. Far from taking pride in being the only one who added some culinary flare to the cafeteria, my stomach twisted with shame because, at that time and in that context, burritos were seen as poor people's food. I remember one time when, as I unwrapped my burrito from the foil, the girls sitting next to me, without asking, started poking the flour tortilla with their grimy fingers and laughing at its texture.

"Ew, gross! It's all soggy and cold!" they shouted across the table, eager to humiliate me.

From that moment on, they nicknamed me "La Juareñita" which to me was a derogatory label that emphasized my otherness, marked by my language, my clothes, my country, my food, and my struggle. From then on, I was no longer interested in fitting in with the other kids at school, and the truth is, there was no time to make friends anyway. When the bell rang at four in the afternoon, it was time to run to the school bus, wait for my mom at my aunt's house, ask for a ride to the bridge, cross the bridge on foot carrying backpacks and grocery bags, walk through downtown Juárez, hop on a *rutera*, and climb the dusty hill. All just to get home around eight, right on time to do homework and eat.

For dinner, my mom served us a plate full of beans and whatever stew she had made that day. I would take a freshly made flour tortilla, spread some beans on it, fill it with the stew, and roll it up to make myself a burrito. As the smell of the stew reached my nose, I would think, "A Juareñita eats better than a little *gringuita*[37]", as I took a bite.

---

[37] Derived from the word "gringo" which how Mexicans refer to people from the United States

Rata de dos patas, gallos con navajas

Two Legged-Rats, Roosters with Blades

Every year, right when June began to peek around the corner, the city would tremble mischievously as its main avenues were decked out with signs laden with double meanings teasing the arrival of the much-anticipated summer bash: *La Expo* of Ciudad Juárez. There was not a single child, parent, uncle, or grandmother who did not get excited by the television commercials announcing the artists scheduled to perform, the endless street food, and the wildest rides of the year. Weeks before the long-awaited event, kids were already saving up their *domingos*[38] so they could roam the fair loaded with ten-peso coins.

La Expo of Ciudad Juárez, a month-long spectacle, was indisputably, for many, the radiant distraction within a sullen reality. It all began with the strategic selection of the site, typically set along the banks of the Río Bravo across from *Avenida del Colegio Militar*, allowing for easy access for Americans who wanted to join the fun. Then, major Mexican celebrities like Vicente Fernández and Ana Gabriel were invited, serving as the main attraction. To make sure children also had their fair share of entertainment, *La Expo* promised a variety of rides for everyone, ranging from

---

[38] Weekly allowances, usually five or ten pesos, handed out on Sundays

carousels for the little ones to flying swings for those seeking a rush of adrenaline.

Despite the collective excitement, which, at least in part, swept me up, too, *La Expo* for us marked the beginning of twisted sleep and a month-long saturation of parties and incessant noise. My parents, serving as the right-hand of the top dogs in Juárez's underworld, had become the heads of the security team at *La Expo*. For that entire month, they were assigned as the main bodyguards for prestigious guests, including those very same celebrities so deeply revered by the public. I confess that writing about it now makes my hand tremble a bit, thinking of just how extraordinary those summers were. What other child could boast to their friends about having met Pedrito Fernández right when his new hit "It Wasn't Me" came out?

It is true that during those stretches of *La Expo* I ran into a myriad of artists, at least in their in-and-out of armored trucks under the cover of night, heads bowed, following my stepfather's instructions to the letter. But I was not amused by such fame. I, like any kid, wanted to ride the carnival rides and eat Juárez-style *elotes* in a cup, where instead of mayonnaise, were spread with a spoonful of butter and sprinkled cotija cheese on top, with your choice of spicy salsa, of course.

After the corn-in-a-cup feast, nothing thrilled me more than the booth with the blown-glass miniatures. While other kids splurged their allowance stuffing themselves with spicy and salty treats, I became obsessed with purchasing glass figurines shaped like animals, tiny flowers, and kitchen utensils. My collection, so I thought, was worthy of praise, seventeen pieces in total, each a different color. So, when I met Paquita la del Barrio, I was carrying a paper cone filled with glass figurines, each one carefully wrapped in more printed news.

To reach the artists' dressing rooms, you had to cross the *palenque*[39], or what I had nicknamed "the butcher's paradise". Beyond the musical acts, food stalls, and carnival rides, the fair proudly swelled around its most attended attraction: the cockfights. A barbarity, no doubt, but an indisputably lucrative one, since the fights were in truth a cover for more illicit dealings. Men in tight cowboy hats and crocodile-skin boots were aroused by the roosters' screams in their battle to survive and the whirlwind of feathers that resulted before their final blow. After the bloody outcome, the shrill whistle of the *palenque* referee would declare a winner, a rooster stripped of feathers, slashed, and limping. A rooster who, after a week, was destined either for the stew pot or to return as the next gladiator of *La Expo*.

It bears mentioning that this spectacle tormented me, and so I made a point to avoid the arena at all costs. Walking beneath the bleachers, it was common to come upon dozens of carcasses bathed in a sheering

---

[39] Arena

purple, all piled up like trash bags without bags. I would shudder at the endless display of greed and the wanton waste of life.

Then, once the bettors' beastly celebration concluded, the sweepers would set about restoring the arena, clearing away every trace of the fight, all to prepare the space for the next act of the night: the concert. At that point, the artists had to be briefed and reminded of their entrance and escape strategies, which they were expected to know by heart. My stepfather led the coordination with the team of bodyguards and made sure to keep the corridors clear of any drunken wanderers or groupies on the prowl for an autograph. When allowed, my mother would take care of the performers' other needs just before they stepped on stage.

That concert night, my mother snuck me into the dressing room, me and my dozen blown-glass figurines. She wanted her eldest daughter to meet the feminist diva of the nineties, the one who had famously dubbed sleazy, cockroach-like men as "two-legged rats". The entrance opened into a room lit by hanging bulbs that, beneath a soot-darkened canopy, offered a feeling of false glamour. On one side of the room stood the mirrors the makeup artists used to beautify their clients; on the other, a white plastic table cluttered with foam cups, bottles of Coca-Cola, and Don Julio tequila. Since I was already bloated from an ill-advised mix of spicy *elote* and cotton candy, the festive scene, a mosaic of booze and cigarette butts strewn carelessly across the table, triggered a sudden stomach cramp.

That feeling of intestinal uproar dissipated the moment I took in the scene that unfolded in the back of the room. Beneath two burnt mustard-colored curtains stitched with silver and gold sequins, the diva awaited us, seated on a made-up bed. Her full figure, adorned in dazzling garments, gave off an air of baroque royalty that drew me in like a magnet. When she saw us walk in, her short yellowish hair lit up, revealing under that same dim light a porcelain-like face and a pair of unforgettable red lips.

Paquita la del Barrio, in all her splendor, smiled and asked, "And who is this little one?"

It was clear that my mother and Paquita already knew each other so I responded, "I am Jacqueline, she is my mom."

"Dear Jacqueline, it is a pleasure to meet you. Will you come watch me when I sing?" she asked.

My intended response was cut short by the slam of the door crashing against the wall across from us. Three bodyguards with an imposing presence stormed in. The men, completely indifferent to me and my mother, looked rushed as they spoke in code to each other and through their radios, intent on taking the diva with them.

"Ma'am, it is time, come with us. Now!" they barked the order without waiting for Paquita to process the sudden masculine commotion that had just invaded her dressing room.

"I am going, but at my own pace, do not rush me," she firmly clarified.

Without pause, courtesy, or consent, and with a hint of arrogance, they yanked her by the arm and slipped through the door. I broke away from my mother and ran after her, shouting, "Paquita! Paquita!" She turned at the sound of my plea and looked at me, closing one eye in a complicit wink that shimmered with her exaggerated lashes and bold blue eyeshadow.

It had not even been twenty minutes before we had already found a gap in the bleachers to watch the concert. Paquita came out onto the stage radiant. Her green dress, lit by the spotlight, flowed with each of her deliberate steps across the platform. I had never heard one of her songs before, but that evening I paid attention to every lyric. My mother, along with the rest of the women in the crowd, sang along in unison to choruses of songs like "Lose Your Respect for Me", "Human Scum", and "I Cheated on You Three Times". I did not see a single man in that crowd as elated about the Mexican diva as the women were.

Back then, I did not know much about men. I did not know about love, or machismo, or femicides, or betrayal. But in witnessing that collective feminine catharsis inspired by a woman who, through her songs full of heartbreak, placed women at the center and reduced men to liars "without spice or salt", I understood three things about Mexican men.

One, men lie. Two, men betray. Three, men kill, sometimes each other, sometimes fighting roosters with blades, sometimes with their own hands... wrapped around a bare neck. Not all men, of course, but always men.

No Need to
Kill Fleas with a Gun

His name was Canelo. We inherited him when we were assigned the house. Canelo was the watchdog of the place, and by taking over as tenants, we had also earned the task of caring for the guardian. Though to be honest, he was not particularly fierce and did not have much of a watchdog personality beyond his deep, authoritative bark. But, as was customary in Juárez, dogs were usually neglected and wandered around in skin and bones. Poor Canelo was also covered in fleas and ticks, and as a result, the whole house felt like a flea-infested anthill.

When we moved in, we did not realize the flea and tick infestation until later. At first, everything was one surprise after another, but of the good kind. The house and its yards, at least in terms of size, left us flabbergasted. It looked like a mansion inside an oasis, surrounded by the chaos of a rowdy city. Enclosed by towering walls, probably about ten meters high, the house was effectively blocked from the sounds of trucks and the blaring music emanating from the booming speakers that drew in the crowds to the many shops along the avenue.

When we first walked in, my mother, her voice tight with emotion, said, "This place feels like a sanctuary".

The building itself looked like one of those abandoned mansions on a hill you see in the movies.

It had three stories, including a damp basement of about two hundred square meters. The main door opened into two rooms, on the left, the living room with a wall painted with a leopard in a jungle, and on the right, a spacious but empty dining room. At the back were the stairs leading to the bedrooms, a wooden kitchen built in the fifties, and a guest room with its own bathroom.

But, just like its dog, the house also lacked some tender, love, and care. Until we arrived, it had only served as a kind of storage. Back then, the police in Juárez were coming down hard with their anti-narcotics raids. We all knew there was no bribe, no matter how stingy, that would not satisfy the authorities, but it was crucial to avoid trouble. So, we were hired to take care of the house, the dog, and the merchandise, playing the role of an ordinary family. Who would suspect that a couple with three small children were neck-deep with the neighborhood's *sicarios*?

"Look, *compadre*, there is always work here, but only count on cash when we pack," the boss explained to my stepfather.

"Damn sure, *compadre*, can't be clearer than water," my stepfather replied.

Our "contract" included only our tenancy in the house, with no additional benefits or salary. For us, the arrangement made sense since we had just gone through a stretch of living in motels and wanted to settle somewhere for a while.

When we moved in, we brought the only belongings we had: our clothes, blankets, a few of my Barbies, and a bicycle. The rest we would have to patiently acquire overtime. As expected, the place did not have a single piece of furniture. We made a bed out of the floor and our blankets and used the stairs as seating. Inside the dusty kitchen cabinets, we found a few burnt pots and a swarm of cockroaches, something that made my mother hysterical.

As soon as we arrived, my siblings and I ran up the stairs, ignoring our mother's resonant warnings; all three of us were in a hurry to explore the bedrooms and claim one for ourselves. I chose the smallest one, the one that connected to an office filled with windows covered in industrial blinds. The only problem with my impulsive choice, something I would learn later, was that from sunrise to sunset, the room was unbearable. The city's harsh and arid summer glare pierced through the blinds and turned the office into an oven.

During the first few weeks, the vastness of that house and its countless corners left to explore filled us with a sense of adventure. But adjusting to a new space, after months of living as homeless squatters, took time. Gradually, we began to see the other side of the coin, the advantages of stability, however modest they could be. Being able to wake up in the same place allowed me to focus on the minutiae of daily life, but since I had never had that luxury before, those routines would have to be stenciled over a clean slate.

My days turned into routine. In the mornings, I practiced riding my bike on my own. After several bruises and the resulting disappointment, I would make breakfast for my siblings. We ate loads of potatoes, submerged in bubbling oil and drowned in ketchup. Then it was time to feed poor Canelo, who at first looked like a sack of bones, though over time, during our stay there, he started putting on some weight. Canelo's greatest issue, however, aside from being malnourished, was that he did not eat for one, two, or three, but for dozens. I never actually counted his fleas, but upon seeing how infested he was, my brother and I turned their extermination into a sort of bug-killing challenge.

As part of our routine, by the afternoon, we would sit on one of the benches in the front yard and begin to de-bug the poor animal from head to tail. Running a hand over his coat, you could feel hundreds of soft bumps. The goal was to part the fur, find a swollen tick, and slowly pull it out with tweezers, careful not to let it burst.

"Gross!" we would scream every time we plucked out a fat bug.

Once it hit the ground, and with great disgust, we would proceed to crush it with one of our sneakers. After the "pop", when we lifted our shoe, there would be a round, violet stain with a little dark dot in the middle. You had to make sure the dark dot got crushed too, otherwise the tick would remain be alive and biting. The genocide sometimes lasted up to an hour. By the time we finished, the sidewalk would be carpeted in bloody footprints, and Canelo would be smiling as if he were proud of his masterpiece.

Aside from that routine, there was not much else to do. The days in that house slipped by, blurring into one another. Inside those walls, it was hard to tell whether it was Tuesday or Friday, since I do not recall going to school during that time. It was a bit easier to recognize the weekends because the morning TV programming aired cartoons like *Hey Arnold* and *Rugrats*. Sundays, on the other hand, were marked by visits from the owners of the house, four young, thin, and sharp-looking guys who always showed up with *barbacoa*, several kilos of freshly made corn tortillas, and two liters of Coca-Cola.

While we prepared our barbacoa tacos topped with cilantro and onion, sitting on the living room floor under the leopard's watchful gaze, the four guys hauled in the gear to get started on the job. The Sunday shift, after breakfast, consisted of walking down to the basement and coming back up with one of the many boxes in storage. Once upstairs, we would empty the boxes filled with dozens of blocks of marijuana wrapped in plastic film. My job was to hand the blocks to one of the boys so he could finish wrapping them with more plastic.

"Do you want to learn how to do it yourself?" one of the four asked me once.

"Only if you teach me and do not get mad," I replied.

Smiling, he proceeded to unroll the film that was secured around a tube and took me by the hand.

"Look, you must grab it from both ends, and I will place the bundle in the middle. Then you wrap it three times," he explained.

Meticulously, I followed his instructions to the letter. I wrapped bundle after bundle three times until, in a matter of minutes, a mountain of tightly packed marijuana bricks, perfectly wrapped, had appeared to keep the feline on the wall company. The task was completed by covering each block with tan-colored tape to mask both its scent and its contents.

"Well then, *mija*, we're going to have to hire you and give you a permanent role, this way we all get rich," said the ringleader of the four visitors, the oldest one.

I blushed at such a compliment. It pleased me to have the approval of the adults, and I felt proud to be a well-behaved girl, even if it meant doing an illicit type of work. Once the Sunday task was done, the four guys packed up their equipment and loaded the bricks into their van. Before pulling away, they handed my stepfather a 500-peso bill with the usual farewell, "Catch you later, *carnal*".

That night we dined like royalty. A taco stand selling *chamorro* had just opened on the corner of the block. The smells were so intense that every day at around seven in the evening, my mouth would start to water in unrelinquished yearning.

It was not enough to survive on ketchup-covered potatoes every day or on *barbacoa* once a week. But that night we treated ourselves to a banquet fit for Mexican gods. As we ate at the steel tables, the kind stamped with the Tecate logo, my stepfather disappeared for a long while. So long, in fact, that by the time he returned, only the last tortilla with a smear of meat was left. But that did not seem to bother him in the slightest. His gaze was distant, and his usual spirited demeanor appeared subdued. This pattern always occurred whenever a bit of money came in, no matter how modest. The rest, in a poetic sort of manner, I already knew by heart.

> Hurry up and let us go.
> Go into the bedroom.
> Turn on the television.
> Do not come out of here.

During those nights of sudden lockdown, rage would devour any traces of my good-naturedness. I could not sleep, thinking about how much I hated him, how with those foolish drunken escapades we were never going to climb out of this crushing misery. I would have preferred anything over seeing him in that muted state. That cursed routine broke my heart at every instance, as if for the first time.

Noticing how my blood, already boiling, had begun to metaphorically evaporate, my ruminating thoughts were abruptly interrupted by my siblings' snores, and I decided, for everyone's sake, to focus on the television instead. During those indecent hours of the early morning, after the national anthem, programming was limited to just a few channels. But on channel thirty-two, my preferred station, I could always find something more or less worthwhile. I fell asleep watching some sort of educational program about water use and waste.

After waking up the next morning, I had an incoherent impulse to save water. I do not know why, but I had to save it. Conscientiously, I tiptoed down the stairs so as not to disturb anyone's sleep and entered the kitchen in full search-and-rescue mode. As part of this unanticipated madness, I needed to find several empty one-liter milk jugs. We only had one, so I chose to improvise and use the two Coca-Cola bottles the four guys had left behind.

With scientific precision, I filled the bottles with water and placed one inside the tank of each of the three toilets in the house. According to the narrators in the documentary, putting a bottle in the toilet helped conserve water because the tank would require less water to flush. I felt proud of my cleverness and went on to begin my routine. The bicycle. The fries with ketchup. Canelo.

A while later, while I was in the middle of the extermination session with a very willing Canelo, I noticed the echoing shouts of my furious stepfather.

"You fucking idiot girl, you bitch! Where the hell are you, you imbecile?!" I heard him yell.

Out of fear, I let a stream of pee escape. With wet pajama pants, I knew what was coming. I hid behind the only tree we had in the front yard. But the yelling got louder, and the rage intensified. I decided to gather my courage and face him. I had clearly done something, and I had to have the guts to show up and take responsibility for my actions, whatever they were.

Slowly, I approached the front door. My hands, still bloody from popping a few fat ticks, grabbed the doorknob and gently turned it to the right. The door opened easily, and there he was, in his underwear looking like a bloated ogre. In one hand, he was holding one of the Coca-Cola bottles I had placed in the downstairs bathroom. When he saw me, he raised his right hand and, with all the skill of a baseball player, hurled the bottle at me. I had no time to run, not even to shield myself from the blow. The bottle slammed violently into my chest and burst.

I ended up soaked in a full liter of water. Without wasting a moment, he launched at me like a rabid dog baring its teeth with the sole purpose of attacking. He threw me to the floor and started kicking me. The shock had numbed me, and the only thing I could register amid the commotion were his insults.

"I am fucking fed up with your nonsense, you little shit!" he yelled as he kept driving his sneaker, laces undone, into my stomach repeatedly.

That is when I heard my mother. She had woken up to the yelling, and when she realized what was happening, she ran out to stop him.

"Let her go, you bastard, you piece of shit, let-her-go...!"

But as she shouted the last syllable, my mother fell down the thirteen stairs that connected the two floors. Lying there on the ceramic floor, completely disoriented and immobilized, she kept begging him through sobs to leave me alone. Finally, he stopped. He looked at me, then at my mother, and walked up the same thirteen stairs she had skipped thanks to her fall. A few minutes later, he came down dressed. Without saying a word, he violently flung the front door open and left.

Frozen by fear and pain, I slowly began to unfurl from my fetal position. I managed to stand up, a bit dizzy, and completely sore, and made the journey across the entire dining room to where my mother lay, nearly incapacitated. During her fall, she twisted one of her ankles. I took her by the arm and managed to lift her off the floor.

"Take me to the *Cruz Verde*[40], *mija*. It hurts so much," she instructed, swallowing back her tears.

We walked two dusty kilometers at a turtle's pace. She, with her right arm over my shoulder. I, with my left arm around her waist, holding her tightly so she would not fall. Not a single car stopped to offer help. The sidewalks between the shops and the highway were uneven and, at times, nonexistent. Every step my mother took, especially over the rockier parts of the route, triggered a feeling of nausea. But she said nothing, she just walked synchronously with the noise of the highway. We finally reached the hospital, covered in dirt and smog. No one asked us what had happened. No one noticed the bruises on my arms. If they did, they kept it to themselves. At the *Cruz Verde*, they had no time for indiscretions. They discharged her quickly. My mother's ankle was put in a cast, and they gave her a prescription. As for me, I was met only with a couple of exhausted stares.

It took my mother exactly a month before she could walk again. We never went back to the hospital to have the cast removed; I slowly broke it off piece by piece. We also ran out of ketchup. The potatoes became just potatoes, submerged in bubbling oil. A week after it all happened, my stepfather returned. No one spoke about the incident, or about where he had been, or with whom. He never asked my mother about her broken ankle either.

---

[40] One of the few hospitals in the city that offered public medical care

Once she regained her movement and her spirit, my mother decided it was time to go, to leave that cursed house, to leave behind all the awful memories. We packed our few belongings into a handful of backpacks, loaded them into the car, and drove off.

We left Canelo with his old owners, the four guys who used to come by once a week to pack up merchandise. Nevertheless, I felt guilty for abandoning him. Who was going to pick off his fleas and ticks now? Who would feed him and the hundreds of tiny tenants living on his back? When we left, he just looked at me with eyes full of resignation. He did not come close; he simply wagged his tail and proceeded to lie down in the shade.

"What's going to happen to Canelo?" I asked.

"Maybe they'll shoot him and get rid of that flea-ridden mess once and for all," my stepdad replied with a laugh.

"But... but there's no need to kill his fleas with a gun. Can we please take him with us?" I pleaded, tears welling up in my eyes.

"Oh, Jacqueline, it's just an expression, don't get all worked up," he said.

Juárez, I have
Unraveled Your Smoke

Juárez,
I have unraveled the smoke
    of your desert,
shaken off
from your earthly crust
that is evanescent
like windblown swirls,
        that roll
like sun-dried tumbleweeds
    and wander with desire
like your hermit scorpions.

 All that remains
  is the faint sting   in my feet
    of your translucent image,
  the ghostly smells of lard
    petrified over your asphalt,
the reflection   of black water
    pooled in the potholes
        of your arteries,
and the humming   of the pachuco
    whose songs
        I no longer remember.

    This is what it means to leave
        and never return
to the place of creed,
    the stolen childhood,
        the sweaty struggle

    beneath the magnifying glass
   that distorts the sun's rays
    the ones that paint
      our eyes black
  and our skin cinnamon.

 Over this departure
   I seal
the spicy sensation
  on my palate,
    that craving,
  out of sheer masochism,
of your flavors
    so full of home.

There is no bridge
    to deter re-entry
      nor wall
 to stomp
  a reunion,
no bible left to read
    to tell the truth,
nor newscast
  to subdue my longing.

Despite such deep seduction,
  I remain,
    with bold irony,
      paralyzed

between this blue
and a goodnight,
      within this place
           so distant
to all that I find near.

End.

ABOUT THE AUTHOR

Jacqueline Loweree (Ciudad Juárez, México, 1989) is a poet, anthropologist, and bipolar woman based in New York City. For over a decade, she has worked in the philanthropic sector leading efforts in evaluation, impact, and social investment across issues such as HIV, housing, and mental health. She is the author of four poetry collections published in Spain and the United States, where she explores intimate themes such as suicide and femicide. Her books include *El tiempo de la mariposa* (2019), *Canciones de una urraca* (2022), *El suicidio del escorpión* (2023), and *De plomo y pólvora* (2024). Throughout her career in social impact, she has collaborated with organizations such as the National Alliance for Mental Illness, the National Institutes of Health, ViiV Healthcare, and Habitat for Humanity International, where she currently serves as a strategist. Her practice, whether through her professional vocation or her writing, weaves together the written and spoken word with social commitment, advocating for justice and empathy.

TABLE OF CONTENTS

No Need to Kills Fleas with a Gun

Autor's Note ·	15
Bundles of Contraband in the 'Gabacho' ·	25
All 'Cause of a Piss, a Burrero ·	41
A Mule in the Hills of Altavista ·	51
The Assassination of Chachito the Goat ·	61
I Don't Want to Die Alone ·	71
Sorrows with Bread (and a Liter of Coke) ·	83
Beware of the Greek God Perverts ·	93
Juareñita 'Americanser' ·	103
Two Legged-Rats, Roosters with Blades ·	115
No Need to Kill Fleas with a Gun ·	125
Juárez, I have Unraveled Your Smoke ·	137
About the Author ·	147

Nueva York Poetry Press

COLLECTIONS

Non Fiction
BREAK-UP
DESARTICULACIONES
Homage to Silvia Molloy (Argentina)

Essay
SOUTH
SUR
Homage to Victoria Ocampo (Argentina)

Non-Fiction
BREAK-UP
DESARTICULACIONES
Homage to Silvia Molloy (Argentina)

Children's Fiction
KNITTING THE ROUND
TEJER LA RONDA
Homage to Gabriela Mistral (Chile)

Drama
MOVING
MUDANZA
Homage to Elena Garro (México)

Poetry

Adjoining Wall
Pared Contigua
Spaniard Poetry
Homage to María Victoria Atencia (Spain)

Barracks
Cuartel
Awards Winning Works
Homage to Clemencia Tariffa (Colombia)

Crossing Waters
Cruzando el Agua
Poetry in Translation (English to Spanish)
Homage to Sylvia Plath (United States)

Dream Eve
Víspera del Sueño
Hispanic American Poetry in USA
Homage to Aida Cartagena Portalatin (Dominican Republic)

Feverish Memory
Memoria de la Fiebre
Feminist Poetry
Homage to Carilda Oliver Labra (Cuba)

Fire's Journey
Tránsito de Fuego
Central American and Mexican Poetry
Homage to Eunice Odio (Costa Rica)

Into My Garden
English Poetry
Homage to Emily Dickinson (United States)

Lips on Fire
Labios en llamas
Opera Prima
Homage to Lydia Dávila (Ecuador)

Live Fire
Vivo Fuego
Essential Ibero American Poetry
Homage to Concha Urquiza (Mexico)

Reverse Kingdom
Reino del Revés
Children's Poetry
Homage to María Elena Walsh (Argentina)

Stone of Madness
Piedra de la Locura
Personal Anthologies
Homage to Alejandra Pizarnik (Argentina)

Twenty Furrows
Veinte Surcos
Collective Works
Homage to Julia de Burgos (Puerto Rico)

Voices Project
Proyecto Voces
María Farazdel (Palitachi)

Wild Museum
Museo Salvaje
Latin American Poetry
Homage to Olga Orozco (Argentina)

INTERNATIONAL POETRY AWARD
PREMIO INTERNACIONAL DE POESÍA NYPP
Award Winning Authors
Homage to Feature Master Poets

For those who, like Silvia Molloy, believe that we write while life still holds—before death or closure settles in—to make sense of a presence turning into absence before our eyes, this book was printed in October 2025 in the United States of America..

www.ingramcontent.com/pod-product-compliance
Lightning Source LLC
Chambersburg PA
CBHW020333170426
43200CB00006B/365